*Critical Bibliographies in Modern History*

# Seventeenth-Century Britain 1603–1714

*Other titles in this series*

**Nineteenth-Century Britain 1815–1914**

David Nicholls (1978)
*(available in cloth and paperback)*

*In preparation*

**Twentieth-Century Britain 1914–70**

Chris Cook & John Stevenson

**Europe 1660–1789**

Hamish Scott

**Europe 1914–78**

Richard Robinson

**British India 1757–1947**

N. Gerald Barrier

*Critical Bibliographies in Modern History*

# Seventeenth-Century Britain 1603–1714

J. S. MORRILL
*Fellow, Lecturer and Director of Studies in History*
*Selwyn College, Cambridge*

DAWSON · ARCHON

First published in 1980



Wm Dawson & Sons Ltd, Cannon House
Folkestone, Kent, England

Archon Books, The Shoe String Press, Inc
995 Sherman Avenue, Hamden,
Connecticut 06514 USA

British Library Cataloguing in Publication Data

---

Morrill, John Stephen
Seventeenth century Britain, 1603–1714.
(Critical bibliographies in modern history;
vol.2
ISSN 0143-6104).
1. Great Britain—History—Stuarts,
1603–1714—Bibliography
I. Title II. Series
016.94106 Z2018 79-91488

ISBN 0-7129-0839-0 cloth

Archon ISBN 0-208-01785-2

Printed and bound in Great Britain
by W & J Mackay Limited, Chatham

# CONTENTS

# PREFACE

The following have read and commented on draft lists of the books discussed below: Drs J. Miller and K. M. Sharpe (chapters 1–4); Dr R. B. Outhwaite (chapters 7–8); Ms M. Heineman and Dr R. S. Porter (chapter 10); Dr P. Jenkins and Mr. M. Ryder (chapter 11). Others have helped by lending me copies of books I wanted to consult and/or discussing particular works with me. I am particularly grateful to Professors D. C. Coleman and G. R. Elton; Drs D. Cannadine, M. Goldie, P. Lake, H. Tomlinson; Messrs J. Hoppit, J. Styles and W. Tighe, and to my research students T. Wales, P. Salt, J. Vage, P. Higgins and P. Hopkins. I am also grateful to Cambridge University Press, Leicester University Press, Open University Press and Oxford University Press for advancing copies of books and other information which helped me to ensure that this book was as up-to-date as possible. None of the commercial publishers I contacted about forth coming titles bothered to reply.

For this, my fifth monograph, my wife has finally retired from the thankless task of turning my chaotic manuscript into a coherent typescript, but her mother, Angela Mead, has shown even greater decoding skills. I am most grateful to her. My wife has, however, put up with even more piles of books and papers about the house than in the past and endured the humours of a broody author with her accustomed fortitude. I dedicate this book to the memory of John Cooper, tutor, mentor and friend, who died in April 1978, just as this book was conceived.

Swaffham Bulbeck, J.S.M.
Cambridge

*Feast of St Matthew*
*1979*

# INTRODUCTION

The most authoritative bibliography of the period 1603–1714 (which lists only books published before 1962 and articles before 1957/8) contains 4,350 principal items and perhaps as many again subsidiary ones. Indeed, as early as 1929, *The Bibliography of Oliver Cromwell* (ed. W. C. Abbott) listed over 3,500 items. In recent years the boom in academic publishing has vastly increased that store of books and articles. The situation for those charged with teaching or learning about this, as any other period of history, is thus a daunting one. In the past three years, during which I have been Tudor–Stuart section editor for the Royal Historical Society's *Annual Bibliography of British and Irish History*, I have had to browse and read some 350–400 items each year. Of these, no more than ten or fifteen have found their way into the reading lists I issue to undergraduates taking the 1450–1750 political and constitutional or social and economic history papers in the Cambridge Tripos. Nonetheless, over eighty per cent of all the titles which I now suggest to students have appeared since I was myself an undergraduate in the mid 1960s.

School-teachers, lecturers and students clearly need guidance about what has been coming out, and about whether some beloved work has stood the test of time. They need to know how to fill particular gaps in their knowledge. The proliferation of project work in undergraduate, college and senior school courses has made this need more imperative. This bibliography attempts to meet those needs. It is a considered selection of the multitude of books on seventeenth-century history in the English language. It is a considered selection but a personal one and it cannot claim to have been made from an omniscient grasp of work in the field. My aim has been to produce a fairly comprehensive review of the publications of the years since the standard bibliography (item **1** below) was produced, and a more limited choice of books from before 1962 which still seem to me neither to have been supplanted nor thoroughly absorbed by the survey literature. It is limited in its scope to a study of the recent secondary literature (there are already good guides to the printed sources, e.g. **1**, **2**, **5**, below). It is assumed that all the books included are of value to those studying history at school, college or university (although 'difficult' and 'technical' works are included with appropriate warning). It is *not* a guide to books readily available or in print, nor is it primarily a guide to the article literature, although *a list* of key articles published in the last twenty years appears as an appendix.

In the remainder of this introduction, I wish to explain the principles of selection and discuss the organisation and nature of the entries. I began by going through the standard aids for this period:

1. G. Davies and M. Keeler (eds.), *Bibliography of British history: Stuart period, 1603–1714* (1970)
2. W. L. Sacshe (ed.), *Restoration England 1660–1689* (1971)
3. G. R. Elton, *Modern historians on British history 1485–1945: a critical bibliography, 1945–1969* (1970)
4. W. H. Chaloner and R. C. Richardson (eds.), *British economic and social history: a bibliographical guide* (1976)
5. G. E. Aylmer and J. S. Morrill, *The civil wars and interregnum: sources for local historians* (1979)

I supplemented my lists from these sources from the Royal Historical Society's *Annual Bibliography of British and Irish History* (annually, 1975+) and from book catalogues from Blackwells (Oxford) for 1967+ and Heffers (Cambridge) 1974+. All this gave me a provisional list of 1,300 titles which I divided up into ten (later eleven) subject groups. I then did some preliminary pruning: carnage was particularly severe amongst the biographies, the local histories and works which upon browsing appeared essentially antiquarian in context. These pruned lists were despatched to the friends and colleagues listed in the preface who made a number of important corrections and suggestions. I then set to work to write the entries. In that majority of cases where I had already read the book, I wrote an entry I thought appropriate. Where I did not already know the work, I browsed or read it in Cambridge University Library. No book discussed below has gone unseen. I checked my impressions and memory against reviews. For this purpose I read all relevant reviews in the following:

*English Historical Review*, 1938–79
*History*, 1958–79
*Economic History Review*, 1958–79
*Journal of Ecclesiastical History*, 1958–79
*Welsh History Review*, 1970–9
*Scottish Historical Review*, 1958–79
*Irish Historical Studies*, 1958–79

*History of Science*, 1962–79

Wherever the reviewer appeared to have been reading a different book from the one I remembered, I went back to the original. I also discovered books I had not come across elsewhere. My work on the Royal Historical Society *Bibliography* allowed me to include all items published up to four weeks before I completed writing this bibliography (i.e. to the end of July 1979). In the event, almost 900 titles were selected for inclusion. I then wrote my final entries. To save space and to allow comparisons, I grouped books on the same or similar fields. The main purpose of the comments is to describe the content of the books, particularly where the title bears little relation to the contents. I have also not hesitated to offer guidance on those aspects of the subject of each book which are particularly thoroughly treated or which have been ignored. A majority of the entries are descriptive but I have praised or criticised works where this seemed to me appropriate. I hope I have not allowed myself too great an indulgence. Indeed, I have tried to reserve my more trenchant opinions for the brief introductory sections at the beginning of each chapter intended to offer an opinion of this strengths and weaknesses of work in that field.

A few further points need to be made:

(*a*) It was very difficult to decide what to do with books which cover a period much larger than the seventeenth century. In general, I have included such books whenever they seem to me clearly to add significantly to our knowledge of that century, even if the relevant section constitutes only a small part of the book. But I have excluded standard works of reference covering long periods (e.g. the *Victoria County Histories*, which contain much information fundamental to the political, administrative, economic, ecclesiastical and educational history of each county). Discovering such works is a notorious problem for bibliographers and I am not sure I have achieved consistency in this regard.

(*b*) Books which reprint articles already published elsewhere have been included on the same principle. They are often more accessible than in their original form. However, I have also included such as were appropriate in the appendix, with cross-references.

(*c*) Although the general principle has been to ignore printed sources, I have made exceptions where it seemed pedantic to impose the rule or where the modern introductions represent the best treatment of the subject in hand.

(*d*) Any arrangement of the books into topics is bound to create anomalies and difficulties. Many works could just as readily be placed in one of several categories – for example Keith Thomas's *Religion and the decline of magic* (**682**) would grace with equal distinction the ecclesiastical, social or cultural history chapters. The solution I have adopted is the most obvious one: to make fairly arbitrary choice and then to signpost the decision with cross-references elsewhere. Not only have I adopted eleven main subject groups, I have also subdivided each. Again this is intended to make the book generally easier to use, but it exerts strains in particular cases. Furthermore, I have adopted different approaches in different chapters. Some chapters – political history, for example – are subdivided chronologically. Others – such as social and economic history – are divided by topic. This may seem inconsistent, but it seemed to me to be dictated by the nature of the scholarship. Political historians are generally concerned to relate different aspects of their subject within a short period, economic historians to follow up one strand over a long period. Indeed, I have found the very process of organising the material instructive. I had intended to treat ecclesiastical history chronologically, but found that to do so would be to cut across the grain of the literature.

(*e*) The entries should be easy to follow. They are preceded by a running number in bold type for ease of reference and cross-reference, followed by the author's name and the main title. I have always given the original date of publication, but have tried to give the date of any later edition which includes major revision. Where a book has been revised several times, I have only given the original date of publication and the most recent revised edition. The nature of the catalogue in the Cambridge University Library is not helpful in this respect, and I may not be very consistent in my attempts to include this information.

Let me add a final note of caution. My own research has made me familiar with the political, administrative and social history of the period as a whole. My teaching experience has given me a fair knowledge of the ecclesiastical and economic aspects as well. But I am not an argus of the Stuart age. My acquaintance with and feeling for intellectual history (chapter 4) is quite limited, for cultural history (chapter 10) vestigial, and for Welsh, Scottish and Irish history (chapter 11) at best patchy. I hope my remarks there are more cautious, and I fear my selection and judgement may be more wayward.

I have found this an instructive and humbling book to write. I have been amazed how many good books I had not even heard of, and have been worried how often my memory of a book read years ago was defective. I hope others will be drawn not only to read new but to re-read familiar works.

*Addenda.* I have taken the opportunity, at proof stage, to add a few additional titles. They appear on pp. 179–180 with the running numbers **A1–A12** and cross-references have been included at appropriate places in the text.

# 1
# GENERAL

The decline and fall of the Whig interpretation of seventeenth-century history is taking some time to be reflected in the more general literature. Indeed, the 1960s and early 1970s, which witnessed a vast expansion in the number of monographs and 'topic' books for students, also induced an unwonted coyness as far as general surveys were concerned. This is now being overcome, with the Paladin histories and the Arnold New History of England series in progress, and a new Oxford History of England series planned. But, for the moment, there is little choice in survey literature. Furthermore, there has been a disproportionate amount of interest in the pre-civil war and mid-century periods at the expense of the Restoration period. This is true both of the volume and the adventurousness of the work produced. A further problem is that apart from those whose interests are essentially economic, virtually no-one appears to be at home on both sides of 1660, which has become as formidable a historiographical divide as 1485 ever was. Above all, no-one has yet found a way of integrating the political and governmental changes of the seventeenth century with the social and economic transformations brought about by population growth and inflation in the century after 1540, while the problems of religion are in general less well comprehended and related to other things than they have been for the sixteenth century. Our knowledge of the religious experience and belief of the people of England for both the periods 1603–40 and 1662–1714 can only be described as sketchy, however much we may know about the battles amongst the intellectuals.

There are three sections in this opening chapter. The first discusses general surveys, that is, books not concerned principally with one particular aspect of the period (politics/society/religion, etc). The second discusses the handful of collections of documents concerned with major aspects of the period as a whole, or several aspects on one part of the century; and the final section draws attention to those collections and essays which deal with a variety of themes.

## Surveys

**6.** R. Lockyer, *Tudor and Stuart England* (1964)

**7.** D. Loades, *Politics and the nation, 1450–1660* (1974)

**8.** C. Russell, *The crisis of parliaments, 1509–1660* (1971)

**6** is simply a very good, effective and clear introductory survey, easily the best thing to give to school and college students to make them feel at home in the period. **7** is also clear and effectively organised around the way the notion of 'good lordship' both strengthened and limited early modern monarchs. The book is running out of steam by the early seventeenth century. **8** is a superb and challenging book ideal for those who already have a firm grasp of essentials. It is equally good on politics, administration and religion.

**9.** J. P. Kenyon, *Stuart England* (1978)

**10.** J. P. Kenyon, *The Stuarts* (1958, 1977)

**9** is the volume Penguin commissioned to replace the disappointing book by M. P. Ashley in its History of England. It is lively, witty, shrewd but too frequently inaccurate. It is very much a political narrative. **10** gives a brief biography of each king, and contains a particularly fine account of the elusive Charles II. Both take the story down to 1714.

**11.** G. Davies, *The early Stuarts, 1603–1660* (1937, 1959)

**12.** R. Ashton *The English civil war, 1603–1649* (1978)

**11** was always amongst the most aldermanic and stuffy volumes in the Oxford History of England and it has only become less digestible with time. The forthcoming appearance of the volume on the same period by Derek Hirst in the Arnold New History of England series will end its useful life. Meanwhile **12** covers most of the period very well. It contains some five analytical (and perhaps slightly static) chapters on the period 1603–40, with five more chapters analysing the events of 1640 in chronological chunks. It contains the best introduction there is to early Stuart religion and culture. Supplemented by J. P. Cooper's chapter 'The Fall of the Stuart Monarchy' in the *New Cambridge Modern History*, vol. 4, this forms the best entry to advanced study of the period.

**13.** G. N. Clark, *The later Stuarts* (1934, 1955)

**14.** J. R. Jones, *Country and court* (1978)

**13** is in the Oxford History of England series and was always a fine example of how to write a magisterial survey of an age: secure, clear, patient and very well indexed. As a narrative, it is supplanted by **14** which in particular contains the only blow-by-blow account of the events of 1688–1714 I have ever found students able to understand. The analytical chapters are just a little less successful, and one longs for chapters on religion and culture.

**15.** G. E. Aylmer, *The struggle for the constitution, 1603–1689* (1963)

**16.** C. Hill, *The century of revolution* (1961)

**17.** D. L. Farmer, *England and the Stuarts* (1961)

**18.** W. McElwee, *England's precedence* (1958)

**19.** S. Brett, *The Stuart century* (1950)

**20.** G. M. Trevelyan, *England under the Stuarts* (1904)

All these are past their prime but all are distinguished in their way. **15** is the most readable straightforward account now available, while **16** combines chronological chapters which are much too brief with vigorous expositions of Hill's distinguished view of the civil war on a class struggle which liberated the English bourgeoisie from the restraints of a reactionary monarchy and made possible the industrial revolution. It is subtle and persuasive but based on a number of premises all subsequently challenged and overthrown. **17–19** are older and more venerable accounts of the rise of liberal democracy of which **20** is the apogee. **20** is still remarkable for its evocation of town and country life, while resounding cadences like 'James I could not distinguish the great currents of opinion and the main tide of political force from the bright, shallow eddies that catch and please a monarch's eye' remind us of the readability, assurance and inadequacy of the Whig historians.

**21.** R. C. Richardson, *The debate on the English Revolution* (1976)

**22.** A. B. Worden, *A Voice from the Watch Tower, Camden Society*, 4th ser., vol. 21 (1978)

**23.** R. MacGillivray, *Restoration historians and the English civil war* (1974)

**24.** F. S. Fussner, *The historical revolution* (1962)

**21** is an undemanding account of changing fashions in the interpretation of seventeenth-century history. It is heavily weighted towards recent work, and its account of earlier histories is not historiography in the proper sense, for which see **22**. This edits a fragment from the original text of Edmund Ludlow's *Memoirs* and, in a long introduction, offers a brilliant reconstruction of the rewriting of the histories and memoirs of the Revolution by Whig and Tory polemicists in the 1690s and 1700s. This in turn weakens the force of **23**, a clear and sensible explication of the attempts made by a great many of those who lived through the civil wars to make sense of their experiences. It takes the story down to the publication of Clarendon's *History* in 1702. Unfortunately it has no thought of going back from the bowdlerised editions of Whitelocke, Ludlow, Hollies, Baxter, etc. to the original texts, and much of what it says is thus vitiated. **24** is an account of the rise of self-conscious historical writing in the sixteenth and seventeenth centuries. There is some overstatement, but the theme is important.

**25.** R. H. Tawney, *Religion and the rise of capitalism* (1926)

**26.** M. Walzer *The revolution of the saints* (1966)

**27.** L. Stone, *The causes of the English Revolution* (1972)

These are challenging and provocative essays which try to relate changing perceptions of man, law and society to economic structures in the early modern period. **25** attempts to anglicise Max Weber, both by stripping him of the jargon which bedevils all sociology, and German sociology most of all, and by being more historically sensitive and responsive. 'Puritanism was the school-master of the English middle classes' remains its elusive motto, just as 'Puritanism was the school-master of the godly magistrates' could be Walzer's. **26** traces the way Calvinism in Switzerland, France and England refashioned the moral imperatives of political elites. Neither can withstand the challenge of detailed recent research. **27** is a bold, vigorous but finally unconvincing attempt to argue for the inability of the Tudor political structure to accommodate or to adjust to changing social forces. The sociologese obfuscates rather than enhances the argument. See the review article, **X33**.

### Documents

**28.** J. P. Kenyon, *The Stuart constitution* (1966)

**29.** E. N. Williams, *The eighteenth century constitution* (1965)

These are companion volumes, dividing at 1688. **28** is an astonishing achievement. The documents are varied, apt, rich, the organisation subtle and economical, the introductions to each section penetrating and crisp: absolutely indispensable. **29** is very straightforward and in fact rather weak on 1688–1715. For this period **37** is a useful supplement, or even alternative.

**30.** G. W. Prothero, *Select statutes and other constitutional documents illustrating the reigns of Elizabeth and James I* (1894)

**31.** J. R. Tanner, *Constitutional documents of the reign of James I* (1930)

**32.** S. R. Gardiner, *Constitutional documents of the Puritan Revolution, 1625–1660* (1889, 1906)

**33.** C. Hill and E. Dell, *The Good Old Cause* (1949)

**34.** S. Prall, *The Puritan Revolution* (1969)

**35.** A. Browning, *English historical documents, 1660–1714* (1953)

**36.** W. C. Costin and J. S. Watson, *The law and working of the constitution, vol. I, 1660–1783* (1952)

**37.** G. Holmes and W. A. Speck, *The divided society, 1694–1716* (1967)

Generations of Oxford students have sweated or dozed through **30** and **32**. Both are models of how to condense statutes and law reports so that the student can gain a knowledge of fundamentals. But both (and this goes for **31** also) select documents to advance the thesis that England was on a high road to civil war under the early Stuarts. **31** is most useful on the neglected projected union with Scotland and on religion. **33** and **34** cover the period 1640–60 and offer generous selections from the radicals as well as the mainstream politicians. **35** has too many snippets and cuts statutes too drastically, but the brief introductions to each section are penetrating. It deals with crown, parliament, finance, the church, provincial life, trade, and the plantations, Scotland and Ireland. I. Roots has a companion volume on 1603–60 in hand. **36** is an austere but well-chosen collection particularly strong on constitutional issues before the courts. **37** (in Arnold's Documents of Modern History) is a wide-ranging survey of Whig and Tory ideas and activities after the Glorious Revolution: readable on its own and an invaluable companion to **29**.

## Collected Essays

This sub-section contains: (i) three volumes of reprinted essays on general themes in seventeenth-century history; (ii) papers presented to, or published in honour of, distinguished seventeenth-century historians or containing a high proportion of seventeenth-century material; (iii) the collected works of major historians. Not included are those collections which bear on a particular field or period within the century, which have been listed in the appropriate chapter.

**38.** K. D. H. Haley (ed.), *The Historical Association book of the Stuarts* (1974)

**39.** E. W. Ives (ed.), *The English Revolution, 1600–1660* (1968)

**40.** P. Seaver (ed.), *Seventeenth-century England* (1976)

**38** collects together the Historical Association Pamphlets which have appeared over the years on seventeenth-century themes. There are not many outstanding ones, but A. M. Everitt on *The Local Community and the Great Rebellion* and K. D. H. Haley on *Charles II* are essential reading. A. M. Woolrych's account of *Penruddock's Rising* (1655) is still the best way into that episode. **39** prints papers which began as radio talks. Three of the six look at provincial responses to the early Stuarts and to the civil war, but the whole book, influential in its time, has been largely superseded by later studies. **40** is another collection of reprints, all readily available elsewhere: L. Stone on social mobility; D. C. Coleman on attitudes to labour, J. H. Plumb on the growth of the electorate, and J. Thirsk on the contrast between the agrarian experience of fielden and upland regions.

**41.** T. Aston (ed.), *Crisis in Europe, 1560–1660* (1965)

**42.** C. Webster (ed.), *The intellectual revolution of the seventeenth century* (1974)

These are collections of essays reprinted from *Past and Present*. **41** includes five varied pieces on seventeenth-century England, with the subjects ranging from notions of monarchy to sectarian women, from alienated intellectuals to the earl of Strafford. **42** reprints twenty-nine pieces clustered around half a dozen subjects: there is a debate about the thought of James Harrington, another about William Harvey, a group of articles on the Levellers and the Diggers, and no less than ten concerned to pin down the relationship (if any) between science, religion and capitalism.

**43.** H. E. Bell and R. Ollard (eds.), *Historical essays* (1963)

**44.** W. Aiken and B. D. Henning (eds.), *Conflict in Stuart England* (1960)

**45.** H. S. Reinmuth (ed.), *Early Stuart studies* (1970)

**46.** D. H. Pennington and K. Thomas (eds.), *Puritans and revolutionaries* (1978)

**47.** P. Clark, A. G. R. Smith and N. Tyacke (eds.), *The English commonwealth, 1547–1640* (1979)

Sadly, not all *Festschriften* live up to the work of their honorand. **43** is for David Ogg and is generally quite successful, though the best articles (C. Hill on 'Propagating the Gospel', H. Trevor-Roper on 'Scotland and the puritan revolution' and P. Laslett on the population of Clayworth and Cogenhoe) have all been reprinted in updated versions elsewhere (in **53**, **54** and **634**). **44** and **45** are far less successful. **44**, presented to Wallace Notestein, is very lightweight and outmoded, though D. H. Willson on James's aspirations for Anglo-Scottish union, M. Campbell on the debate about overpopulation and W. Aiken on the unhappy Admiralty Commission of 1679–84 are still useful. **45**, for D. H. Willson, contains nine slender essays on narrow subjects, with only W. J. Jones on the politics of Lord Chancellor Ellesmere and J. K. Gruenfelder on the Short Parliament election retaining value. By contrast, the Christopher Hill *Festschrift* **46** is an excellent one. Few of the authors reach conclusions their honorand would have looked for, but all address themselves to his sort of question and nine or ten of them are now basic reading for the period. **47** honours Joel Hurstfield and contains a liberal proportion of Stuart studies, of which A. G. R. Smith on the Great Contract, C. Russell on Pym in the 1620s and A. Hassell Smith on the militia statutes (or lack of militia statutes) are outstanding.

**48.** F. J. Fisher (ed.), *Essays in the economic and social history of Tudor and Stuart England* (1961)

**49.** J. Thirsk (ed.), *Land, church and people* (1972)

**50.** C. H. Chalklin and M. Havinden (eds.), *Rural change and urban growth, 1500–1800* (1975)

**51.** D. C. Coleman and A. H. John (eds.), *Trade, government and economy* (1976)

**48** is an outstandingly good and varied collection on 'Tawney's Century, 1540–1650' of which J. Thirsk's study of industry in the countryside and D. H. Pennington on 'the accounts of the kingdom' 1642–9 are models of their kind. R. Ashton, D. C. Coleman, G. E. Aylmer and L. Stone donated important offshoots from their major works, while C. Hill is at his most elegant on protestantism and the rise of capitalism. **49** is the *Festschrift* to H. P. R. Finberg, published as an *Agricultural History Review* supplement. It contains three key articles for the period, all developed at greater length by their authors elsewhere: J. Thirsk on the contrast between sheep–corn and woodland–pasture rural communities; M. Spufford on the schooling of the peasantry; V. Skipp on the economy of the Forest of Arden. **50** is the *Festschrift* to W. G. Hoskins. Seventeenth-century specialists will be most drawn to J. Thirsk on tobacco-growing and C. H. Chalklin on new towns. **51** honours F. J. Fisher, and seven of its thirteen chapters concern us. R. Ashton on the conflict of concessionary interests (domestic and overseas), P. Corfield on urban growth and N. Harte on sumptuary legislation are of wide significance, and the editors' own contributions on the Anglo-French commercial treaty of 1713 and grain exports after 1660 are also excellent.

**52.** H. R. Trevor-Roper, *Historical essays* (1957)

**53.** H. R. Trevor-Roper, *Religion, the Reformation and social change* (1967)

**54.** C. Hill, *Change and continuity in seventeenth-century England* (1974)

**55.** C. Hill, *Puritanism and revolution* (1958)

**56.** G. R. Elton, *Studies in Tudor and Stuart politics and government* (2 vols., 1974)

**57.** J. Hurstfield, *Freedom, corruption and government in Elizabethan England* (1973)

**58.** W. G. Hoskins, *Provincial England* (1965)

**59.** J. H. Hexter, *Reappraisals in history* (1961)

**60.** G. Davies, *Essays on the later Stuarts* (1958)

**61.** C. H. Firth, *Essays, literary and historical* (1938)

**52** is a collection of forty-two miniatures in 300 pages, culled mainly from the *New Statesman* and the *Times Literary Supplement.* **53** is a collection of nine substantial reprints, including a study of 'Oliver Cromwell and his parliaments' and of Dury, Comenius and Hartlib, foreign philosophers in the English Revolution. **54** reprints thirteen pieces of which the pieces on the critics of the professions and on the 'Many-headed monster' (i.e. gentry fears of the mob) are the best. **55** is an older collection of fourteen pieces, mostly adumbrating later work on religious radicalism, but containing Hill's fullest treatment of the myth of the Norman Yoke and of the agrarian legislation of the revolution. **56** and **57** are mainly Tudor essays, but G. R. Elton's discussion of the Apology of 1604 and much of his writing on parliament is of great interest for the later period, as is J. Hurstfield's piece in **57** – reprinted from the *V.C.H.* – on Wiltshire government. **58** is mainly pre-seventeenth century but includes the famous piece on the rebuilding of rural England, 1570–1640 (but see now article **X375**). **59** includes a famous rebuke to all participants in the controversy over the rise of the gentry and an elegant piece on parties within the Long Parliament. **60** consists of three posthumous essays – 'Charles II in 1660' (a wide-ranging and harsh judgement on the king), 'Tory churchmen and James II', and 'the control of British foreign policy by William III'. The second and third have been superseded by recent work. **61** consists of seven essays, six of them on the Stuart period. Four offer penetrating assessments of Raleigh, Milton, Clarendon, and Burnet as historians, the first and last of which have never been bettered (for Clarendon see now **163**, and for Firth's longer treatment of the *History of the Great Rebellion*, see his article in *English Historical Review*, 1904). There are also interesting essays on Bunyan and on the political significance of *Gulliver's Travels.*

**62.** L. S. Sutherland (ed.), *Studies in history* (1966)

**63.** I. R. Christie (ed.), *Essays in modern history* (1968)

**62** is a collection of nine famous British Academy lectures, including W. Notestein's 'winning of the initiative by the House of Commons', R. H. Tawney's 'Harrington's interpretation of his age', and F. J. Powicke on Spelman's 'Concilia'. **63** reprints key articles from the *Transactions of the Royal Historical Society* and includes five seventeenth-century items, including F. J. Fisher's on London as a centre of conspicious consumption and H. Phillips's on the last years of Star Chamber.

# 2
# GOVERNMENT

The overall picture here is very patchy. A number of quite outstanding monographs in recent years have transformed our understanding of aspects of Stuart government – e.g. the works by Aylmer (**82, 94**) and Roseveare (**98–99**) – but we are still very dependent on the work of scholars fifty or a hundred years ago. Their weaknesses are principally a tendency to view administration from the administrators' perspective and a rather myopic concern with their own institutions, so that the relationship between separate institutions is very hard to uncover. Many important financial and legal bodies are largely unstudied. No one has gone beyond the handful of leading cases to examine the work of the principal common law courts (King's Bench or Common Pleas). Chancery and Requests are unexplained beyond 1620, and our knowledge of Star Chamber really rests on one outdated, and two obscure, articles (**63, X4–5**). Detailed knowledge of the internal workings of the financial bodies is equally obscure, certainly for the period up to 1670. But most breathtaking is the lack of any institutional study of parliament. We think we know a great deal about the 'political' wrangling between the king and the two houses, but next to nothing about parliamentary procedure and about the fundamental function of parliaments: lawmaking.

One further weakness can be noted particularly in the first section. Historians much prefer to write the history of one institution over a long period than all institutions over a short one. We urgently need a new general account of the institutions of Stuart England, particularly since the political historians are so keen to maintain that these broke down in the early part of the century, were never the same again, and were then revamped after the Glorious Revolution. Furthermore, there is no easy way of discovering how the various central institutions – legal, financial, military, etc. – combined, let alone how the institutions of central and local government functioned together. For these questions we have to turn to very detailed monographs and local studies. Most of the books in the first section are as arid as it is possible for history books to be.

## General Works

**64.** W. S. Holdsworth, *A history of English law* (13 vols., 1922–1952)

**65.** E. G. Henderson, *Foundations of English administrative law* (1963)

**64** is encyclopaedic and judicious. Its careful assessments are not always as thorough as they seem, however, and many of the perspectives have obviously been changed by subsequent research and changes of interest, but it is absolutely fundamental for every aspect of the law. Volumes IV to IX go under the collective title 'the Common Law and the king, 1484–1700', but volumes V and VI are the crucial ones. **65** is a very short book on a subject less grand than its title but still of importance. It studies the development in the period 1600–1750 of two writs (*Certiorari* and *Mandamus*) which gave the subject access to the courts when he experienced injustice at the hands of government officers.

**66.** E. R. Turner, *The Privy Council of England from 1603 to 1784* (2 vols., 1927)

**67.** E. R. Turner, *Cabinet councils of England in the seventeenth and eighteenth centuries* (2 vols., 1930)

**68.** F. M. G. Evans, *The principal secretary of state, 1580–1680* (1923)

**69.** M. Thomson, *The principal secretary of state, 1680–1783* (1932)

**66** and **67** are both very long and very solid but do not always see the wood for the trees. Both volumes of **66** are relevant, but only the first volume of **67** is so. Cabinet councils are seen as growing out of committees of the Privy Council, hence the coverage from 1622. Turner was only concerned with the institutional history – thus very dull if essential reading. **68** (often catalogued under Miss Evans's marital name of Higham) combines a biographical approach with an analysis of the tasks of the secretaries. It is very much an institutional study again, but sharper and clearer than **66–7**. **69** is shorter, organised topically, but quite crisp. It is difficult to disentangle the later Stuart parts. See also **A69** (p. 179).

**70.** J. P. Dawson, *A history of the lay judges* (1960)

**71.** W. H. Bryson, *The equity side of Exchequer* (1975)

**70** is a curiously organised but very important book which examines the work of Chancery, the commissions of the peace and manorial courts, particularly in the early modern period. Plucknett described the equity side of Exchequer as 'by far the most obscure of all English jurisdiction', but in **71** it receives a very austere and careful analysis. The bulk of the book is concerned with the period from 1570 to 1714.

**72.** J. S. Cockburn, *A history of English assizes, 1558–1714* (1972)

**73.** J. H. Langbein, *Prosecuting crime in the Renaissance* (1974)

**74.** J. H. Baker (ed.), *Legal records and the historian* (1970)

**75.** J. H. Langbein, *Torture and the law of proof* (1978)

**72** is a magisterial survey of the judicial, administrative and political aspects of the assize judges' work. **73** contains a detailed study of the Marian statutes on bail and committal, and argues that seventeenth-century J.P.s acted as examining magistrates both in drawing up the evidence upon which indictments were drawn and in taking witnesses through their evidence at the trial. **74** is a collection of essays based on conference papers, and one of them – J. S. Cockburn's on the wide discrepancies between trial theory and practice – casts some doubt on parts of **73**. Other seventeenth-century chapters in **74** look at Star Chamber litigants, attorneys in King's Bench and Common Pleas, and at counsellors' fees and the earnings of Sir Edward Coke. Over half of **75** deals with England's 'century of torture' from 1540 to 1640 through a detailed analysis of eighty-one surviving torture warrants. It dispels certain misapprehensions and compares English and continental practice. See also **673–7**.

**76.** W. Kennedy, *English taxation, 1640–1799* (1913)

**77.** E. Hughes, *Studies in administration and finance* (1931)

**78.** E. Cannan, *A history of local rates* (1896)

**76** is a short study of the 'grounds of English tax policy', particularly of the distribution of taxation amongst the population. It relates tax theory to political theory. **77** is a rather relaxed and discursive history of the regulation of the salt industry and is as important for its discussion of the question of salt patents before 1640 as it is for the administration of salt excises thereafter. **78** is another short study of the rating system in early modern England which considers the effects of rating occupiers as against owners of property. It is still both indispensable and readable.

**79.** S. and B. Webb, *English local government from the Revolution to the Municipal Corporations Act* (9 vols., 1906–29)

**80.** J. H. Gleason, *The justice of the peace, 1560–1640* (1969)

**81.** W. Tate, *The parish chest* (1940, 1969)

**79** is supposed to cover the period 1688–1834, but draws liberally from earlier sources. Vol. 1 on *The parish and the county*, and vols. 2 and 3, *The manor and the borough*, are the crucial ones and still basic. **80** is disappointing, being under-researched and unimaginative. It examines the membership of the commissions of the peace in six counties in six scattered years and seeks out changes in such things as the social and educational background of J.P.s. It has one brief chapter on the burdens of office. **81** is a successful textbook produced by an experienced W.E.A. lecturer and is intended to introduce newcomers to the ecclesiastical and civil records of English parishes. It does its job well.

## 1603–1642

**82.** G. E. Aylmer, *The king's servants: the civil service of Charles I, 1625–1642* (1961)

A book of the utmost importance. It describes the structures of the Household, the departments of state, the law courts, and so on, examines the social structure of office-holding and conditions of service and discusses the political role of office-holding and office-holders. It is now complemented by a parallel volume on the 1650s (**94**).

**83.** H. E. Bell, *An introduction to the history of the Court of Wards and Liveries* (1953)

**84.** J. Hurstfield, *The Queen's Wards* (1958)

**83** is a straightforward, clear account of the working of the Court of Wards from its creation in the 1530s to its demise in 1646. **84** looks at the fate of its clients down to the death of Salisbury in 1612.

**85.** W. J. Jones, *The Elizabethan Court of Chancery* (1967)

**86.** L. A. Knafla (ed.), *Law and politics in Jacobean England* (1977)

**87.** L. M. Hill (ed.), *Sir Julius Caesar: The Ancient State, Authority and Proceedings of the Court of Requests* (1976)

**88.** G. C. Squibb, *The High Court of Chivalry* (1959)

**85** treats the personnel and procedure of Chancery down to the death of Egerton in 1618; it is not easy to read. **86** is an edition of eight of Egerton's tracts, prefaced by a 200-page introduction which includes a strong section on the movement for law reform in the early years of the century. Both contain important discussions on the clash of jurisdictions. The introduction to **87** treats Requests less successfully, but it is the only thing available. **88** contains an interesting chapter on the earl of Arundel's role in the revived Court of Chivalry in the 1630s.

**89.** W. Prest, *The inns of court, 1590–1640* (1972)

**90.** B. P. Levack, *The civil lawyers in England, 1603*–42 (1973)

Two lucid and wide-ranging books. **93** examines the recruitment, training, and ideology of the common lawyers, and **90** treats the civil lawyers (a much smaller group) even more broadly, paying particular attention to their role in 'politics'. Both revise accepted opinions. Work on a third key group, the attorneys, by C. Brooks, is in hand and will be appearing soon.

**91.** L. Boynton, *The Elizabethan militia, 1558–1638* (1967)

The last hundred pages are specifically on the early Stuarts and much of the rest is relevant. It needs some revision in the light of subsequent local studies (e.g. **694**, **695**, **705**, article **X406**), but is a very good introductory survey. See also **100**.

**92.** E. R. Foster, *The painful labour of Mr Elsyng* (1972)

**93.** C. G. C. Tite, *Impeachment and parliamentary judicature in early Stuart England* (1975)

**92** is an account (published by the *American Philosophical Society*) of the work of the early Stuart clerk to the parliament, Henry Elsyng, in particular his authoritative study of *The Manner of Holding Parliaments.* **93** is partly a political study of the revival of 'impeachment' in the 1620s, but it is mainly an attempt to show the differences between fourteenth- and seventeenth-century theory and practice.

## 1642–1660

**94.** G. E. Aylmer, *The state's servants: the civil service of the English Republic, 1649–1660* (1973)

**95.** R. Sherwood, *The court of Oliver Cromwell* (1977)

**96.** M. A. E. Green (ed.), *Calendar of the Committee for Compounding* (5 vols., 1889–93)

**94** is a magnificent study to complement **82**. Once again Aylmer describes the institutional structure, the terms of service, the social biography and the politics of the office-holders, though his attempted comparison with the pre-war royal servants is unconvincing. **95** shows how kinglike were the trappings of Protectoral power. There are no other books specifically on the institutions of the 1640s and 1650s, though some political histories do contain administrative chapters (this is particularly true of local studies, for which see **180, 181, 182, 695, 709, 710, 711, 712, 716**). See also **216**. **96** contains, in volumes 1 and 5, long introductions on how parliament administered the estates of its defeated enemies.

## 1660–1714

**97.** S. Baxter, *The development of the Treasury, 1660–1702* (1957)

**98.** H. Roseveare, *The Treasury, 1660–1870* (1973)

**99.** H. Roseveare, *The Treasury: the foundation of a British institution* (1969)

There is no equivalent for this period to Aylmer's books on the 1630s and 1650s. The best introduction is a chapter by Tomlinson in **228** which he intends soon to expand into a short book. **97** and **98–9** have rather different views on the increasing control exercised by the Treasury and both should be read. **98** is a full-length monograph, **99** a hundred-page survey, plus illustrative documents. See also **611, 612**.

**100.** J. R. Western, *The English militia in the eighteenth century* (1965)

**101.** W. R. Ward, *The land tax in the eighteenth century* (1953)

**102.** P. M. Fraser, *The intelligence of the secretaries of state, 1660–1688* (1955)

**100** and **101** both start back in the seventeenth century and examine important problems in the relationship of local and central government. **100** is too heavily based on central records, and **101** needs to be supplemented by article **X7**, but both are readable and reliable. **102** looks at the use of spies, at naval intelligence during the Dutch wars, and at the secretaries' control of government propaganda through the London *Gazette*. A diffuse but engrossing book.

**103.** F. A. Jacobson, *William Blaythwayt* (1932)

**104.** G. W. Keeton, *Lord Chancellor Jeffreys and the Stuart cause* (1965)

**105.** J. Beresford, *The godfather of Downing Street: Sir George Downing* (1925)

**106.** P. S. Lachs, *The diplomatic corps under Charles II and James II* (1965)

**103** is an outstandingly good portrait of an administrator of the new style in the Restoration period. Blaythwayt was secretary at the War Office from 1683 to 1704. **104** claims that historians have misjudged Judge Jeffreys, and its advocacy is quite plausible if long-winded. Downing deserves a more fully researched biography than he receives in **105**, which is prolix and tiresomely vague on an important diplomat and treasury reformer, prominent in both the 1650s and 1660s. **106** is a clear and entertaining account of a skeleton service run on a shoestring!

# 3
# POLITICAL HISTORY

Even after the ruthless excision of countless superficial and romantic biographies, this chapter contains more titles than any other. That does not mean that this aspect of the period is better understood or more comprehensively covered. Indeed, it is one of the most patchily treated. It is astonishing how few themes have been followed through for the century as a whole: a glance at the first section will show the scale of the problem. Within each period within the century, the strengths and weaknesses are very different. Taking the periods 1603–42 and 1642–60, the discovery of local history (that there is a political world, a political consciousness, away from Whitehall and Westminster, and that the art of politics in the seventeenth century largely consisted in harmonising the discrepant political expectations and aspirations of central government and provincial political nations) has proved an enormous stimulus in recent works. Such an approach would certainly transform our understanding of the period after 1660 but it has yet to be taken up by historians. Even the very best work, such as **14**, **228**, **258** and **279**, suffers from an absence of this perspective. Parliamentary history is also comprehensively covered both for the early Stuart and post-1689 periods, but far more needs to be done on the period 1653–1689.

On reflection, the previous sentence fell into a very common trap. Parliamentary history is *not* well known: only the history of the House of Commons is well known. Just how far that distorts our perspective it is difficult to say, but there are some suggestions that the distortion is very considerable. C. Russell has recently written, with great perception: 'the difficulties of the early Stuarts were not difficulties with their parliaments: they were difficulties which were reflected in their parliaments'. Hitherto, parliamentary history throughout the century has been written too much in terms of its own internal dynamics without reference to other political worlds. We are beginning to learn something of the provincial background to elections and to parliamentary business. We still know far too little about the formal and informal political activities at court. Here, the success of political biographies for the Restoration give them the advantage, but for the period 1603–42 far too little work has been done on the precise ways in which individual ministers and courtiers worked together and against one another. A history of the high politics of the period of the kind so familiar to students of eighteenth or mid-nineteenth to early-twentieth-century politics would both be useful in itself and be invaluable in further unravelling the complexities of parliamentary history. The 1640s are bedevilled by heroic but foolish attempts to impose order on chaos, to find a key to the political behaviour of men whose consistency, if it existed at all, was not of the kind imagined by those inured to modern party or caucus politics. The patient and involved *context* delineated in **195** for the period 1649–53 probably applies earlier. The 1650s are a dark decade. We know far too little about the role of the army, about the councils of state, about the internal dynamics of the Protectorate parliaments. We have a lot of very detailed studies, and a lot of very general stuff. Broadly conceived and thorough studies of innumerable subjects are now called for (e.g. the nature and effectiveness of government propaganda; the nature and consequences of the military presence in the provinces; the activities of the army council; the work of the council of state under the protectorate; the legislation of the Protectorate parliaments; the changing nature of English republicanism between the early and late 1650s).

After 1660 the position reverses itself: quite a lot is known about high politics, very little about low politics, about local politics, about the relations of centre and provinces, about electoral history. Virtually no serious effort has been made to *analyse* patterns of continuity and discontinuity from the civil war years into the Restoration. Yet the high politics is quite well covered, particularly through the appearance of a large number of very scholarly and indeed definitive biographies. The best of these, e.g. **243**, **245**, **246**, **288** and **290**, surpass anything from the early seventeenth century. There is good work on Cranfield, adequate, if unchallenging, recent works on Cottington and Portland (and excellent ones on Laud and Stafford now overtaken by recent work), but nothing recommendable on Robert Cecil, Buckingham, Pym, Eliot, Haselrig, Fairfax or Lambert, to name only those for whom a wealth of material is available. The only figure of comparable stature after 1660 lacking a thorough modern biography is Clarendon.

Let me end this lament on a more positive note. Two books in chapter 1 now offer a very clear and sound narrative of the politics of the period (**8** supplemented by **12** for 1603–60 and **14** for

1660–1714), while five collections of essays in Macmillan's Problems in Focus series (**123**, **150**, **193**, **228**, **273**) provide challenging reassessments of many of the more ticklish problems. Between them they cover the whole of our period excepting the 1640s, a gap which will be filled with the appearance of J. S. Morrill (ed.) *Reactions to the English civil war*, probably in 1982.

## General Works

**107.** G. M. D. Howat, *Stuart and Cromwellian foreign policy* (1974)

**108.** P. Langford, *The eighteenth century* (1976)

**109.** J. R. Jones, *Britain and Europe in the seventeenth century* (1966)

**107** and **108** are complementary volumes in the Modern British Foreign Policy series published by A. & C. Black. **107** covers 1603–1688, **108** 1688–1815. The introductory chapter to **108** on 'foreign policy and its setting' is particularly useful. Both are essentially chronological surveys of 'the conduct of British foreign policy'. **109**, which concerns 1603–1714, is briefer, more analytical and more lively than **107**. It is in Arnold's Foundations of Modern History series.

**110.** K. Feiling, *A history of the Tory party, 1640–1714* (1924)

This is a classic work which still offers one of the most thoughtful and subtle accounts of the rise and fall of ministries in the years between 1660 and 1714, although a good deal of the conceptual framework has been dismantled by more recent histories. In some ways, however, it remains the best study of the continuities of Tory thought through the 1688–9 vortex.

**111.** L. G. Schwoerer, *No standing armies!* (1973)

This is a discussion of anti-army ideology from the early to the late seventeenth century, with a heavy emphasis on the standing army debates in parliament in the late 1690s. The other interesting section is on the militia ordnance debates of 1641–2, for which see article **X163**.

**112.** J. Cannon, *Parliamentary reform, 1640–1832* (1973)

This contains only two rather impressionistic chapters on the period 1640–1715, but they are the best available, apart from article **X143** (but see also **130** and **X167**). Like the rest of the book, they are witty and stimulating.

## 1603–1642

**113.** S. R. Gardiner, *A history of England from the accession of James I to the outbreak of the civil war* (10 vols., 1864–86)

**114.** C. V. Wedgwood, *The king's peace, 1637–1641* (1955)

**113** remains *the* authority and *the* indispensable narrative. Returning to it after some years I was amazed by the moderation and carefulness with which Gardiner unfolds the coming of the Puritan Revolution. It is far less 'whiggish' and presumptuous than Trevelyan **(20)**, for example. **114** is a reliable and sensible narrative of events between the opening of Charles I's struggle with the Scots and the end of the first phase of the Long Parliament.

**115.** D. H. Willson, *James VI and I* (1956)

**116.** S. J. Houston, *James I* (1973)

**117.** D. Mathew, *King James I* (1967)

**118.** D. Mathew, *The Jacobean Age* (1941)

**119.** A. Fraser, *King James VI of Scotland, I of England* (1974)

**120.** W. McElwee, *The wisest fool in Christendom*

**121.** G. P. V. Akrigg, *Jacobean pageant* (1962)

**122.** R. Ashton, *James I by his contemporaries* (1969)

James I has found his biographers too fastidious to observe the ability and farsightedness that lay behind the tawdry lifestyle. Some other recent books and articles suggest that a major reappraisal and upgrading of his kingship is called for. Meanwhile **115** is the standard biography, with a stern judgement on the king's abilities. The treatment is broad and manages to be both chronological and topical at once. Two-thirds of it deal with the period after 1603. For most purposes, however, **116** is a far better, shrewder, incisive account of the reign. It is in Longman's Seminar Studies series and is only one-third the length of the others. Beyond these two books, little is recommendable. **117–18** are both idiosyncratic in their treatment of the king, questions of religion and culture dominating and problems of government and of the crown's finances getting short and inaccurate shrift. But **117** does contain a good introductory study to James's writings and **118** is a deeply felt evocation of the age. **119–20** are simply bland, dull 'life and times'. **121** is a bulky series of essays built around the book's subtitle – *The court of James I* – but chapter headlings like 'tears for Prince Henry' and 'the marriage of Thames and Rhine' belie the serious scholarship underpinning the book. For most people, however, the best introduction to James I would be to read **115** or **116** and then to move on to **122**, a readable and wide-ranging anthology, disappointing only in its skimped quotations from James's own writings.

**123.** A. G. R. Smith (ed.), *The reign of King James VI and I* (1973)

This is a collection of essays in Macmillan's Problems in Focus series. The treatment of James VI is livelier than the treatment of James I, with a regrettable absence of anything on the English church, but there are excellent chapters on the crown and the courts and on local government as well as a wide-ranging introduction.

**124.** C. H. Carter, *The secret diplomacy of the Hapsburgs, 1598–1625* (1964)

**125.** M. Lee, *James I and Henry IV* (1970)

Two recent studies which illuminate English relations with the Catholic powers. **124** covers Hapsburg relations with many parts of Europe in a rather unsystematic way, but includes an excellent study of Spanish intelligence reports about the court of James. **125** is more cogent and, although restricted to the years 1603–10, it examines the diplomatic relationships between the two monarchs, and the consequent effect on their relations with Spain, the Netherlands and Germany.

**126.** W. Notestein, *The winning of the initiative by the House of Commons* (1924)

**127.** W. B. Mitchell, *The rise of the revolutionary party in the House of Commons, 1604–1629* (1950)

**128.** D. H. Willson, *Privy Councillors in the House of Commons 1604–29* (1940)

**129.** K. M. Sharpe (ed.), *Faction and parliament* (1978)

**130.** D. Hirst, *The representative of the people?* (1975)

**126–8** broadly represent the traditional view of the growing self-assurance and power of the House of Commons. They are practical studies of the institutional aspects of this growth (see **27**,

**298, 306–7** for the ideological aspects). This interpretation has been coming under increasing attack, particularly from Professors G. R. Elton and C. S. R. Russell (see **56, 135** or article **X158**). Now **129** offers a collection of essays modifying our understanding of the working of parliament and offering new perspectives on the behaviour of the members. The introduction and the chapter by D. Hirst on court and country attitudes are outstanding. The latter is a pendant to **130** which overturns our understanding of the size and behaviour of the electorate, which is shown to have been large, frequently unmanageable and far from passive.

**131.** W. Notestein, *The parliament of 1604–1610* (1971)

**132.** T. L. Moir, *The Addled Parliament* (1958)

**133.** R. Zaller, *The parliament of 1621* (1971)

**134.** R. E. Ruigh, *The parliament of 1624* (1971)

**135.** C. Russell, *Parliaments and English politics, 1621–29* (1979)

**131–4**, each by an American scholar, dwell on 'political' issues and assume England is on a high road to civil war, though **132** is of interest for the way it demonstrates that the failure of the 1614 parliament was largely the consequence of the intra-governmental feuds spilling over into parliament, and **133** concentrates on the foreign-policy problems. **135** offers a wholly persuasive new perspective and a depth of scholarship far beyond the respectable level achieved in the others. Russell shows how parliament failed to meet the political and fiscal challenge of the decade. The first eighty pages offer an analysis of the English political system which is required reading for any understanding of the period. This is followed by a lengthy account of each parliamentary session in turn, but the narrative is far more fluent and clear than anything approached in the other works. The speculative conclusion on the relationship between the events of the 1620s and the civil war-to-come is simply brilliant and whets the appetite for Russell's forthcoming volume in the 'New Oxford History of England'.

**136.** M. Prestwich, *Cranfield: politics and profit under the early Stuarts* (1966)

**137.** R. H. Tawney, *Business and politics under James I* (1958)

Cranfield alone amongst James's servants has found a convincing biographer. **136** is a vast book, broadly conceived as a 'life and times' and contains not only a clear account of its subject's public career, but the best general survey of the formal and informal structure of Jacobean government. **137** is an extended essay or set of essays on aspects of the financial and commercial world of the period. Both are highly recommended.

**138.** J. Epstein, *Francis Bacon, a political biography* (1977)

**139.** J. Marwil, *The Trials of Counsel* (1976)

There are a number of books on Bacon's 'scientific method' and mentality (see **785–6**), but these two are the only serious studies of his public career. **138** is a very straightforward, unadorned biography, less penetrating and suggestive than **139**. On the other hand **139** is rather awkward in its organisation (it sees Bacon's *History of Henry VII* as a personal credo which can unlock his political career). Both take old-fashioned whiggish views on the political background and therefore, to my mind, distort the significance of Bacon's career.

**140.** C. D. Bowen, *The lion and the throne* (1957)

**141.** S. D. White, *Sir Edward Coke and the 'Grievances of the Commonwealth', 1621–1628* (1979)

**140** is a general study of the lawyer, royal councillor, obstreperous M.P. and supposed champion of Whiggish liberties. It shrinks from a study of the legal records and is better as a sustained account of his doings than an appreciation of his mind, values or achievements. **141**, although it concentrates on just one aspect of Coke's career – in the parliaments of the 1620s – is much more satisfying and finds him to be a man disenchanted with the existing administration but without any commitment to deep structural change. It largely but not wholly endorses the views of **135**. There is also an outstandingly good general appreciation of Coke's career at the beginning, and the whole book is a triumph of clarity and judiciousness: an important work.

**142.** K. M. Sharpe, *Sir Robert Cotton, 1586–1631* (1979)

**143.** A. G. R. Smith, *Servant of the Cecils: The life of Sir Michael Hickes, 1543—1612* (1977)

These are biographies of secondary figures. **142** is a book of great importance, however, for the subject allows the author to offer a brilliant study of the intellectual milieu of the period, and of the nature and utility of seventeenth-century antiquarianism. It greatly strengthens the view of early Stuart politics propounded in other recent studies, notably **129** and **135**. **143** is a more modest volume, the last third of which covers Hickes's activities as a minor court official, as money-lender and confidant to Salisbury in the early years of the century. See also **A11** (p. 179).

**144.** B. White, *Cast of ravens* (1965)

**145.** W. McElwee, *The murder of Sir Thomas Overbury* (1952)

**144** is the best of several accounts of the greatest court scandal of the period, but **145** is also very readable. For most purposes, however, curiosity about the affair will be slaked by the account in volume 2 of **113**, which also contains a documentary appendix.

**146.** J. Bowle, *Charles I* (1975)

**147.** D. R. Watson, *The life and times of Charles I* (1973)

**148.** D. Mathew, *The age of Charles I* (1951)

**149.** R. Strong, *Charles I on horseback* (1972)

There is no satisfactory biography of this most private of kings. **146** makes good use of contemporaries' comments and offers a sympathetic portrait of Charles in the 1620s and 1630s, but loses sight of his man in the 1640s. Bowle also blurs and oversimplifies constitutional issues. **147** is well-illustrated but even more superficial. **148** is impressionistic and episodic but often deeply satisfying. **149** is a study of Charles' self-image as expressed in Van Dyck's portraits. It perhaps ought to belong to chapter 10 of this book, but can come in here and should be looked at by teachers and bright students at an early stage, pending an adequate biography (at least two major ones are in preparation). See also **A6** (p. 179).

**150.** C. Russell (ed.), *The origin of the English civil war* (1973)

**151.** P. Zagorin, *The court and the country* (1969)

**152.** W. J. Jones, *Politics and the bench* (1971)

**153.** R. Ashton, *The city and the court, 1603–42* (1979)

**154.** V. Pearl, *London and the outbreak of the Puritan Revolution* (1964)

**150** is an excellent series of essays in the Problems in Focus series. N. R. N. Tyacke's chapter on religion in the 1630s, C. Russell's on parliament and the king's finances and P. W. Thomas's on court culture are fundamental. **151** is more dated than it looks, because it was written several years before it appeared and its attempt to apply a 'court–country' polarity to the period has been widely seen as so oversimplified as to be unhelpful. **152**, in the

Historical Problems: Studies and Documents series, is hard to read but worth the effort for its insight into the use of the courts by the early Stuarts. The relevant chapter in **72** is shorter and almost as useful. **153** is a highly original treatment of the relations of the city of London and of the court, adumbrated in chapter 4 of **12**. It modifies **154** which retains great value, however, particularly on 1641–2. See also articles **X28** and **X351.**

**155.** M. F. Keeler, *The Long Parliament, 1640–1* (1954)

**156.** D. Brunton and D. H. Pennington, *Members of the long Parliament* (1954)

**155** gives a brief biography of every M.P. and a report for every constituency. **156** attempts a group profile of royalist and parliamentarian M.P.s and of the recruiters returned in 1645–7. It finds few differences between supporters of king and parliament except their average age. See also articles **X28** and **X351.**

**157.** C. V. Wedgwood, *Thomas Wentworth, earl of Stafford* (1961)

**158.** J. H. Timmis, *Thine is the kingdom: the trial for treason of Thomas Wentworth, earl of Stafford* (1977)

**157** is a heavily rewritten version of an earlier biography. It is sound and clear. **158** uses fresh evidence in the House of Lords Record Office, but vitiates its discoveries by spurious psychologising about 'inventive creating phases' and 'justifying motives'. See also **838**, articles **X37**, **X74**, **X465** and an article to appear in *Northern History* by P. Salt on Wentworth's parliamentary career.

**159.** M. van C. Alexander, *Charles I's lord treasurer* (1975)

**160.** M. Havran, *Caroline courtier: the life of Lord Cottington* (1973)

**161.** H. Hulme, *The life of Sir John Eliot, 1592–1632* (1957)

**162.** J. Adair, *A life of John Hampden* (1978)

**163.** B. H. G. Wormald, *Clarendon* (1951)

**164.** J. H. Hexter, *The reign of King Pym* (1941)

**165.** S. R. Brett, *John Pym: the statesman of the English Revolution* (1943)

**159** fails to grasp the complexity of Stuart fiscal records but is a reasonable survey of court intrigue in the early 1630s. Its treatment of Caroline parliaments, however, has now been superseded. **160** is reasonable on Cottington's diplomacy, but is very conventional and lightweight on politics and administration. **161** is tedious and uncritical: for Eliot see now the article by J. N. Ball in **129** or his Cambridge Ph.D. thesis (1955). **162** is a disappointing political biography by a distinguished military historian. **163** is an incomplete masterpiece, a study of Clarendon as politician and historiographer. Part I is fundamental to any elucidation of the politics of 1640–2. **164** looks at Pym's genius as political operator and administrative improvisor in 1641–3. Russell's article on Pym in the 1620s (**X47**) whets the appetite for the fuller treatment promised. Meanwhile **165** is a milk-and-water life with no body to it. See also **A4** (p. 179).

## 1642–1660

**166.** E. Hyde, Earl of Clarendon, *History of the Great Rebellion* (6 vols., 1702, 1888, 1958; several other editions)

**167.** H. R. Trevor-Roper (ed.), *Selections from Clarendon* (1978)

**168.** S. R. Gardiner, *History of the great civil war 1642–1649* (4 vols., 1893)

**169.** S. R. Gardiner, *History of the Commonwealth and Protectorate* (4 vols., 1903)

**170.** C. H. Firth, *The last years of the Protectorate* (2 vols., 1909)

**171.** G. Davies, *The restoration of Charles II* (1955)

In general this book is not concerned with original sources, but **166** is so basic, so readable, so much better an account than most other things, that it would be ludicrous to omit it. School and college students will not have time for the whole thing, so a new selection, **167**, will be most useful for them. It should be mandatory. **168** and **169** constitute the standard authority and though the conceptual framework has been challenged (above all in the treatment of parliamentary affairs) it remains unshakeable as a balanced narrative. Gardiner did not live to take the project beyond the election to the 1656 parliament and Sir Charles Firth took the story on to the death of Cromwell (**170**). Many years later, Firth's pupil completed the project down to 1660 in a rather lacklustre volume (**171**).

**172.** I. Roots, *The Great Rebellion, 1640–1660* (1966)

**173.** C. V. Wedgwood, *The king's war, 1641–7* (1958)

**172** is the best recent narrative, balanced, clear and witty: in fact, the only recommendable brief account of the 1650s. **173** is a skilfully assembled record of the parliamentarian victory. See also **12**, **348** and **349** for accounts of the course of the war itself.

**174.** B. S. Manning, *The English people and the English Revolution* (1976)

**175.** B. S. Manning (ed.), *Politics, religion and the English civil war* (1973)

**174** examines the role of popular movements in bringing about the civil war. It is overwhelmingly concerned with the twelve months from October 1641 and is strongest on events in London. Its central argument has been vigorously challenged by most reviewers, but the final chapters on the ideas of the Levellers as the heir of the popular movement have been more warmly welcomed. It must also be said that the writing is very congested, and most students get more out of the articles (**194**, **X119**) and out of the two chapters by the editor in **175**, which also includes contributions by several of Manning's former research students. The chapter by C. Davis on the Levellers and Christianity is a most important piece.

**176.** D. Underdown, *Pride's Purge* (1971)

**177.** J. R. MacCormack, *Revolutionary politics in the Long Parliament* (1973)

**178.** M. Kishlansky, *The rise of the New Model Army* (1979)

**179.** C. H. Firth, *The House of Lords in the civil war* (1910)

Ever since the old division of the Long Parliament into presbyterians and independents as presented by S. R. Gardiner was challenged in the 1930s, the internal dynamics of that body in the 1640s has been a source of dismay and ill-temper for historians (e.g. **59**; articles **X65**, **X68–71**, **X130**, **X132**, **X138–9**). **176** is easily the best attempt to impose a fresh order on chaos. It offers an account of the developments in the Commons which parallels developments in the provinces and then follows the story through the climacteric of December 1648 into the Rump. It is a book to be read by anyone seeking to come to terms with the period 1646–53. **177**, on the other hand, is over-schematic, incoherent and profoundly unconvincing. **178** is as much about parliament as about the army. Its attempts to demythologise the saints in arms is deeply satisfying; but it too is over-schematic on parliament itself. A forthcoming study of Denzil

Holles by P. Crawford promises to clarify things, but more work is urgently needed on the Lords. Meanwhile there are many plausible and many more implausible suggestions in **218**, and a few illuminations in **176**. Otherwise it is back to **179** (which actually covers the period 1603–60 elegantly but skimpily).

**180.** J. S. Morrill, *The revolt of the provinces* (1976)

**181.** C. Holmes, *The Eastern Association in the English civil war* (1975)

**182.** D. H. Pennington and I. A. Roots, *The committee at Stafford, 1643–5* (1965)

**180** examines provincial reactions to the government of Charles I and to the onset of civil war, emphasises the nature and extent of neutralism and also analyses the consequences of a civil war on English institutions and political values. **181** is an excellent case study of how the resources of the parliamentarian heartland were harnessed to the war effort, emphasising that even there support for the parliament was far from uniform or unequivocal. **182** looks at parliamentarian organisation in a divided county. See also several books in chapter 9 (**695**, **709–716**).

**183.** G. E. Aylmer, *The Levellers in the English Revolution* (1975)

**184.** H. Shaw, *The Levellers* (1968)

**185.** A. S. P. Woodhouse, *Puritanism and liberty* (1938, 1950)

**186.** H. N. Brailsford, *The Levellers* (1961)

**187.** J. Frank, *The Levellers* (1944)

**188.** M. A. Gibb, *John Lilburne, the Leveller* (1946)

**189.** P. Gregg, *Freeborn John* (1961)

**190.** M. Ashley, *John Wildman, plotter and postmaster* (1947)

**191.** W. Schenk, *The concern for social justice in the Puritan Revolution* (1948)

Books on the Levellers are innumerable, but this selection should cover the whole range of opinions about them. **183–4** are excellent brief introductions, **183** being more incisive and with generous if abbreviated readings across the range of Leveller political thought, while **184** in Longman's Seminar Studies is a less satisfactory blend. **185** is a critical edition of the Putney debates and a mass of supporting material, together with a hundred page introduction discussing the place of the Levellers at one wing of the disintegrating Puritan tradition. **183–5** make a reading of **186**, long-winded, overstated and with its heart on its sleeve, largely redundant. Go straight to **187**, a fine and probing discussion of the development of Leveller thought. **188** is shorter and less up-to-date than **189**, but is shrewder and more convincing as an intellectual biography; both are readable. **190** looks at the long and curious career of Wildman after, as well as during, his involvement with the movement. **191** offers a series of clear sensible explications of the thought of the Levellers, Diggers, Fifth Monarchists and other radical groups. There is much else on the Levellers, but I think more is to be gained by moving sideways to the relevant sections in **174**, **175**, **193**, **455**, **462** than back to older histories like those of T. C. Peace (1916), D. B. Robertson (1951) or H. Holorenshaw (1939).

**192.** C. V. Wedgwood, *The trial of Charles I* (1964)

This is a pendant to **114** and **173**, a stirring and telling narrative of the regicide.

**193.** G. E. Aylmer (ed.), *The interregnum* (1972)

**194.** R. H. Parry (ed.), *The English civil war and after* (1970)

**193** is a distinguished series of essays in Macmillan's Problems in Focus series. The various pieces are less well integrated than in sone other volumes in the series, but the standard of individual essays is very high: K. V. Thomas on 'the Levellers and the franchise', J. P. Cooper on 'the social and economic problems of the Commonwealth', C. Cross on the church and D. Underdown on 'settlement in the provinces' are all fundamental reappraisals of their subjects. **194** is a modest collection aimed at sixth-formers (the papers began life as lectures to the Oxbridge set at Eton). A. Woolrych on Barebones Parliament and I. Roots on the major-generals are foretastes of larger works to come and are the best introductions to these topics available.

**195.** A. B. Worden, *The Rump Parliament* (1974)

**195** is a brilliant reconstruction of the politics of the Rump and a masterly appraisal of its achievements. It should also be read for its persuasive portrait of Cromwell. There is as yet nothing at all comparable on the Barebones or Protectorate parliaments, although work on the former by A. Woolrych and on the latter by P. Pinckney is well advanced.

**196.** P. H. Hardacre, *The Royalists during the Puritan Revolution* (1956)

**197.** D. E. Underdown, *Royalist conspiracy in England, 1646–1660* (1960)

These books complement one another. **196** is not so much about the royalists as about the policies and practices of their victorious opponents towards them. It is an important study of the processes of sequestration and composition (i.e. the confiscation of royalist estates and their return on payment of heavy fines) and of the major-generals. **197** explores the reasons why royalist conspiracies were so ineffectual and finds the reasons in the divisions within the exiled court, in the English provinces and in the brilliance of Cromwell's intelligence service.

**198.** C. Korr, *Cromwell and the New Model foreign policy* (1975)

This is a disappointing work, and is in fact only about Anglo-French relations. The most stimulating recent work on Cromwellian foreign policy is the article by Crabtree in **205**, but see also article **X149**.

**199.** C. H. Firth, *Oliver Cromwell and the rule of the puritans* (1900)

**200.** R. S. Paul, *The lord protector* (1955)

**201.** H. E. Lovell Cocks, *The religious life of Oliver Cromwell* (1960)

**202.** R. Howell, *Cromwell* (1976)

**203.** C. Hill, *God's Englishman* (1970)

**204.** J. Buchan, *Oliver Cromwell* (1934)

There are innumerable biographies of Oliver Cromwell. I would be very surprised if he was not the most biographied Englishman. But few of them begin to come to terms with him. Despite its age, **199** is still the most satisfying all-round account. No-one since Firth has had such an intimate knowledge of the main memoirs and political correspondence of the period, much of which he had edited. **200** is a thorough and clear life, often praised for its treatment of religious themes, but on that I prefer the little known **201**, very short and based only on the most obvious sources, but somehow plumbing the inwardness of Cromwell's faith. **202** is also a readable and clear portrait, but it misses some of Cromwell's passion and overstates his intelligence and consistency. Those with a fair grasp of the period, or who have read **199**, can proceed straight to **203**, a commentary on Cromwell's life rather than a narrative, full of interesting points and acute observations. It also has an outstanding chapter on Cromwell's notion of divine providence which is reprinted in **205**. There are innumerable popular narratives, including fairly recent ones by M. Ashley, A. Fraser and C. V. Wedgwood, but the unadorned and elegant one by Buchan, **204**, remains my own favourite. For two military biographies see **363–4**.

**205.** I. Roots (ed.), *Cromwell: a profile* (1973)

**206.** M. Ashley (ed.), *Great lives observed: Cromwell* (1969)

**205** is a most successful reader, reprinting a number of key articles, including H. R. Trevor-Roper's on Cromwell and his parliaments and R. Crabtree's reassessment of his foreign policy. **206** offers a series of extracts from Cromwell's own writings and from his and our contemporaries. It is well done. Cromwell revealed a great deal of himself in his writings and speeches. All but pedants will use the freely available edition by T. Carlyle rather than the modern one by W. C. Abbott, with its dull and anachronistic commentary.

**207.** E. M. Hause, *Tumbledown Dick* (1972)

**208.** R. W. Ramsey, *Richard Cromwell* (1935)

**209.** R. W. Ramsey, *Henry Cromwell* (1933)

**207** is a rambling and often dubious reassessment of the second lord protector, but offers good reasons why we should question the circumstances of Richard's accession. Ramsey's biographies of Cromwell's sons (**208–9**) are straightforward, unexceptionable and unexciting.

**210.** V. Snow, *Essex the rebel* (1971)

**211.** M. A. Gibb, *The lord general* (1938)

**212.** W. H. Dawson, *Cromwell's understudy* (1942)

**213.** M. Ashley, *General Monck* (1977)

**214.** R. W. Ramsey, *Henry Ireton* (1949)

**215.** J. Berry and S. G. Lee, *A Cromwellian major-general* (1938)

Six political biographies of military men. **210** is thoroughly sympathetic and well worth reading on Essex. It does well to relate his early humiliations in the Jacobean court to his later career as parliamentarian general and moderate politician. **211** is less satisfying on Fairfax, indeed bitterly disappointing from the author of so good a life of Lilburne (**188**). **212** makes a strong case for Lambert as the ablest practical thinker of the 1650s, and as the man behind most of Cromwell's successes. See also Heath in article **X79** and in **205**. **213** gives a lucid account of Monck's career but his mind and reasoning remain obscure. Ireton emerges less satisfyingly from **214** and deserves a better biography. **215** is an excellent study of James Berry, a secondary figure. It offers refreshing perspectives on the politics of 1647, on the army's benefits from the sale of crown lands in the early 1650s, and on the activities of Berry, major-general for Wales, 1655–7.

**216.** V. Rowe, *Sir Henry Vane the Younger* (1970)

**217.** R. Spalding, *The improbable puritan* (1975)

**218.** G. F. T. Jones, *Saw-pit Wharton* (1967)

Not many civilian parliamentarians have been adequately biographied, probably because so few left any private papers and because of the shortage of parliamentary diaries from the Interregnum. Vane has been the subject of some breathtakingly bad books, but **216** is very sound, particularly in its analysis of Vane's work as a naval administrator. **217** offers a very straightforward and unsurprising account of Bulstrode Whitelocke, based on a return to the original text of his writings which reveals the inadequacy of the editions everyone else has relied on. **218** is a perverse account of a perverse man, whose public career spanned the period 1640–90. The book rightly concentrates on the 1640s, and makes some very interesting suggestions about the importance of the House of Lords in that decade. However, at times it makes sense of the man by reinterpreting the times too freely.

**219.** F. Jessup, *Sir Roger Twysden* (1965)

**220.** P. W. Thomas, *Sir John Berkenhead* (1969)

**219** is a pleasant study of the sufferings of a gentle and honourable soul buffeted by the events of 1640s, and examines the public career and private intellectual pursuits of this Kentish gentleman. **220** is even better as a study of the royalist wit and polemicist. One regrets the lack of a comparable study of his parliamentarian counterparts (e.g. Marchamont Nedham).

**221.** W. Parker, *Milton: a biography* (2 vols., 1968)

**222.** D. M. Wolfe, *Milton and the puritan revolution* (1941)

**223.** A. Barker, *Milton and the puritan dilemma* (1942)

**224.** C. Hill, *Milton and the English revolution* (1977)

**221** is an immensely thorough biography. Volume 1 contains a 300,000-word life, volume 2 even more wordage in notes, discussion and appendices. **222** is an intellectual biography which concentrates on Milton's social thought and on the years 1640–60. **223** is a neglected study of Milton's conception of society and of the conflict between individual liberty and justice, religious freedom and order. **224** is the most challenging and stimulating. I find its discussion of Milton's later poems as an attempt to come to terms with a God who has betrayed his chosen people very satisfying, more so than its view of the austere scholar picking up ideas from the radicals in the alehouse.

## 1660–1689

**225.** J. Thirsk (ed.), *The Restoration* (1976)

**226.** P. Morrah, *Restoration England* (1979)

**227.** D. Ogg, *England in the reign of Charles II* (1934)

**228.** J. R. Jones (ed.), *The restored monarchy* (1979)

**229.** J. Miller, *Popery and politics, 1660–1688* (1973)

**230.** H. Nenner, *The judiciary and politics, 1660–1688* (1976)

**231.** J. Levin, *The Charter controversy in the city of London, 1660–1688* (1969)

The best general introductions to Restoration are **13–14**. **225** is a collection of readings from contemporary and recent writings about the settlement itself, with a good introduction. The only weak section is the one on religion. **226** is a book which evokes life in Restoration England and looks at the lifestyle of courtiers and countrymen, at life in cathedrals and in brothels, at high culture and low culture: thinly researched but vigorously written. **227** is, deservedly, a classic: lucid, broadly conceived, Whiggish, invaluable not so much for its political narrative as for its chapters analysing institutions and structures. **228** is a collection of eight essays plus introductory survey in the Problems in Focus series. The treatment is rather old-fashioned and unadventurous but the chapters on finance and administration, and on the law and the constitutions, are both excellent digests of some very solid and tedious monographs, and the chapters on foreign relations and on trade and shipping are now the best introductions available. **229** is not a book on catholicism but on anti-popery and is excellent as much. **230** is weak and built around a flimsy central thesis. For almost every purpose, the shorter accounts in general works are preferable. **231** considers both the legal and political problems of the crown's interference with the charters of London and considers the wider political implications of the ensuing conflict.

**232.** M. Ashley, *Charles II* (1973)

**233.** C. Falkus, *The life and times of Charles II* (1972)

**234.** M. Ashley, *James II* (1978)

**235.** J. Miller, *James II: a study in kingship* (1978)

**236.** F. Turner, *James II* (1948)

**237.** P. Earle, *The life and times of James II* (1972)

Charles II has eluded his biographers almost as fully as his father has done, though **232–3** both offer creditable, if lightweight, surveys of the reign. James II has been more fortunate. Of the two recent biographies, **234** is much to be preferred to **235** for scholarship and cogency. It also offers a surprisingly adverse judgement on Charles II's political skills. But the 'revision' of James's objectives will not convince all, and these should turn still to the old and reliable **236**. **237** is one of the more successful of the Kings and Queens of England series, and is lavishly illustrated.

**238.** T. H. Lister, *The life and administration of Edward, 1st earl of Clarendon* (3 vols., 1837–8)

**239.** Sir H. Craik, *The life of Edward, earl of Clarendon* (2 vols., 1911)

**240.** D. R. Lacey, *Dissent and parliamentary politics, 1660–78* (1969)

**241.** D. Witcombe, *The Cavalier House of Commons* (1966)

**242.** M. Lee, *The Cabal* (1965)

The absence of a serious work on Clarendon's period as lord chancellor forces us back either on general works or on the old accounts like **238** and **239** The latter is supplementary, less valuable, and should not be taken on its own. Volume 3 of **238** contains correspondence from 1660–7 and is a better introduction to Clarendon himself than his bitter, inaccurate and shapeless autobiography, a sad appendage to the glorious *History*. **240** is long, thoroughly researched, rather dull to read, but it contains, in a very useful appendix, the brief biographies of all M.P.s sympathetic to dissent. **241** is a short account of the relations of crown and parliament in each parliamentary session between 1661 and 1674: a mini-Neale. **242** is an untidy book, examining the period 1667–74, not chronologically or topically, but by taking the role of each member of the Cabal in turn. The book, like its subject, thus lacks coherence.

**243.** K. D. H. Haley, *The first earl of Shaftesbury* (1967)

**244.** C. H. Hartman, *Clifford of the Cabal* (1937)

**245.** A. Browning, *Thomas Osborne, earl of Danby and duke of Leeds* (3 vols., 1944–51)

**246.** J. P. Kenyon, *Robert Spencer, earl of Sunderland* (1958)

**247.** H. C. Foxcroft, *The character of a trimmer* (1946)

**248.** J. P. Kenyon, *Halifax: complete works* (1969)

Most of the heavyweight politicians of Charles II's later years have found good biographers. **243** is a remarkably controlled, detailed and satisfying narrative of a most tortured career, replacing all its predecessors, but it does not get to the heart of the man. **244** is an underrated study of an overrated and disagreeable lord treasurer, with an important set of his letters as an appendix. **245** is a definitive, straitlaced study of the Tory first minister of Charles II and William III. The documentary appendices are massive and of great importance. **246** is simply the best biography of anyone in our period, a book which illuminates both the man and his times. Spencer held high office under Charles II, James II and William III and possessed none of Danby's consistency. **247** is a life of the Marquis of Halifax by an author who did not really comes to terms with her subject's intellectual range, eclecticism or ultimate consistency. The introduction to **248** goes some way to redress the balance but a lengthy reappraisal is awaited.

**249.** J. M. Wallace, *Destiny his choice: the loyalism of Andrew Marvell* (1968)

**250.** E. Heath-Agnew, *Roundhead to royalist* (1977)

Biographies of two secondary figures whose careers as parliamentarians-turned-royalists bear a superficial resemblance only. **249** is a penetrating study of the poet, polemicist and administrator, and it finds a consistency in his conduct important for our understanding of others than Marvell. **250**, by contrast, is a lightweight but readable study of the career of Colonel John Birch, presbyterian officer in the west in the 1640s, overt Cromwellian in the 1650s and active supporter of the restored monarchy. He served in every elected parliament between 1646 and his death in 1691.

**251.** J. R. Jones, *The first Whigs* (1961)

**252.** J. P. Kenyon, *The Popish Plot* (1972)

**253.** F. S. Ronalds, *The attempted Whig revolution of 1678–1681* (1937)

**254.** P. Earle, *Monmouth's rebels* (1977)

There is scope for more studies of the Exclusion Crisis, particularly beyond the bounds of court and parliament. A reappraisal of toryism would be particularly welcome. Meanwhile, **251** is an excellent survey of the rise and fall of Shaftesbury's ramshackle alliance, and **252** a very readable and convincing reappraisal of Oates, his fabrications and the trials that ensued. It almost makes Lord Chief Justice Scroggs an attractive figure. **253** is really superseded, but has some use for its comments on individual Whigs. **254** looks at the 1685 rising to thwart James, and is particularly strong in its analysis of who supported Monmouth and why.

**255.** P. Geyl, *Orange and Stuart, 1641—1672* (1969)

**256.** K. D. H. Haley, *William of Orange and the English opposition, 1672–4* (1953)

**257.** K. Feiling, *British foreign policy, 1660–1672* (1930)

**255** (which is a translation of a work largely written by 1935) is a rather curious work examining how two royal houses helped and (more usually) hindered one another in adversity. It is more concerned with the Dutch than the English 'angle': a rather hard-going narrative. **256** is a searching reassessment of the political background to the Third Anglo-Dutch war, making extensive use of Dutch archives. **257** is rather flowery and moralistic, but also lucid and full in its discussions of the tergiversations of royal policy.

**258.** J. R. Western, *Monarchy and revolution* (1972)

**259.** J. R. Jones, *The revolution of 1688 in England* (1972)

**260.** J. Carswell, *The descent on England* (1969)

These three works complement one another very neatly and

between them provide a satisfying account of the downfall of James II and of the nature of the Glorious Revolution. **258** and **259** both emphasise the growth of royal power in the 1680s and the essentially limited objectives of James II. **258** treats the decade as a whole, while **259** is clearer in delineating the phases of James II's blind march to humiliation. It also emphasises the continental dimension, but less fully and clearly than **260.** All three are attractively written.

**261.** M. Ashley, *The Glorious Revolution of 1688* (1966)

**262.** S. E. Prall, *The bloodless revolution* (1970)

**263.** L. Pinkham, *William III and the respectable revolution* (1954)

**264.** G. M. Trevelyan, *The English Revolution, 1688–9* (1938)

**261–2** are straightforward narratives which portray James's actions and motives much too crudely. **263** puts all the emphasis on William's personal ambitions and on the narrow self-interest of the English peerage. It trivialises the revolution unacceptably. **264** is a classic account, encapsulating Macaulay's whiggery and libertarianism and is now of mainly historiographical interest (though there is some remaining value in the chapter on Scotland).

**265.** D. Hosford, *Nottingham, the nobles and the north* (1976)

This is the only local study which deals with late-seventeenth-century politics, exploring the background to the rising in the north midlands during the Revolution. It combines this with a general review of the behaviour of the peerage. The two approaches are not very well integrated, and the book is under-researched, but the intention was good and it should find vigorous imitators.

## 1689–1714

**266.** D. Ogg, *England in the reign of James II and William III* (1957)

**267.** G. M. Trevelyan, *England under Queen Anne* (3 vols., 1930–4)

**266** is a sequel to **227**, and is generally held to be less compelling, probably because it is more crudely teleological. It remains the classic moderate Whig view of the Revolution. **267** is rather hard-going nowadays, but it is still unrivalled as an account of the progress of the war, and, to a lesser extent, of the diplomacy.

**268.** S. Baxter, *William III and the defence of European liberty* (1965)

**269.** J. Miller, *The life and times of William and Mary* (1975)

**270.** N. Robb, *William III* (2 vols., 1966)

**271.** H. Chapman, *Mary II* (1953)

**272.** D. Green, *Queen Anne* (1970)

**268** is an outstanding and sympathetic royal biography which benefits enormously from its use of the Dutch archives. **269** is a straightforward and well-illustrated volume in the Kings and Queens of England series, less scholarly than the author's life of James II (**235**) but perfectly sound. **270** is simply rather dull, and inferior to **268** in everything but length. **271** is a rather touching if lightweight portrait of an increasingly morbid queen. **272** is a very clear reappraisal of Mary's sister, and finds her tougher, more wilful and far less stupid than the legend. The background is, however, hazy and often inaccurate.

**273.** G. Holmes (ed.), *Britain after the Glorious Revolution* (1969)

**274.** J. H. Plumb, *The growth of political stability* (1967)

**275.** L. Glassey, *Politics and the appointment of justices of the peace, 1675–1720* (1979)

**273** is an outstanding collection of essays in the Problems in Focus series and contains an excellent anti-Whig view of the 1689 settlement by J. Carter, pioneering studies of the nature and function of parties by H. Horwitz, L. E. Ellis and G. Holmes, and of the Church by G. V. Bennett. **274** are J. H. Plumb's justly famous Ford Lectures in Oxford, learned, cogent and influential. They have been modified by later work, but are still fundamental. **275** is a book expressly inspired by those lectures which concludes by modifying Plumb's views. It examines all exclusions from and additions to the commissions of the peace for the fifty plus counties of England and Wales and establishes the political contexts within which the changes took place, and the political influences which shaped those changes. It is a very dry and cautious book, but an illuminating one.

**276.** H. Horwitz, *Parliament, policy and politics in the reign of William III* (1977)

**277.** D. Rubini, *Court and country* (1967).

**276** is a difficult book to assess. It is immensely well-researched and detailed, and all the specialists have reviewed it enthusiastically. Yet I have found it (as have my unwarned undergradutes) indigestible and exhausting as a blow-by-blow account of parliamentary history. The three analytical chapters (4, 9, 13) certainly offer clear and penetrating analyses of post-revolutionary politics, but I find the rest unreadable. **277**, which eschews the Whig–Tory dichotomy in favour of a court–country one as the dynamic, organising principle behind politics in the 1690s, is also hard-going, but I have found it worthwhile and more arguable than its critics have allowed.

**278.** R. Walcott, *English politics in the early 18th century* (1956)

**279.** G. Holmes, *English politics in the age of Anne* (1967)

**280.** W. Speck, *Tory and Whig* (1970)

Few books have suffered a greater pulverisation by its critics than **278**, an attempt to namierise the 1700s. The assault led by **279** is by and large effective, but **278** still needs to be read if the other books on the period are to be understood. **279** is a quite outstanding achievement, panoramic, secure, clear and brilliantly organized. It anatomises politics at court and in parliament, and finds the Whig–Tory dichotomy to be the key. **280** is a slender book which finds party organisation and ideology at the heart of electoral history.

**281.** B. W. Hill, *The rise of parliamentary parties, 1689–1742* (1976)

This book offers a chronological account of high politics from the Revolution to the fall of Walpole. For the period after 1715 it is both clear and shrewd (particularly on the survival of toryism) but the earlier part is rather congested and lacking in narrative distance. **14** is to be preferred.

**282.** R. Hatton and J. S Bromley (eds.), *William III and Louis XIV* (1968)

**282** is a rather unusual *Festschrift* (for M. Thomson). Published posthumously, it combines essays by several of his pupils and friends with reprints of his own excellent articles. The chapters on the personal relations of the two kings, on parliament and foreign policy, on the succession question and on English newspapers in the 1690s are particularly important.

**283.** G. H. Jones, *The mainstream of Jacobitism* (1954).

**284.** G. H. Jones, *Charles Middleton: life and times of a Restoration politician* (1958)

Jacobitism in the first twenty-five years after 1689 is a very neglected subject, and certainly **283**, based sensibly but unsubtly on the most obvious sources only, is no substitute for a full study, which should include analysis of the French archives. **284** is excellent on the drudgery and routine of Middleton's time as James's junior secretary while he was still on the throne, but is very hazy and thin on the former's more prominent time at St Germain.

**285.** J. O. Richards, *Party propaganda under Queen Anne* (1972)

**286.** J. A. Downie, *Robert Harley and the press* (1979)

**287.** G. Holmes, *The trial of Doctor Sachaverell* (1972)

**285** is a very straightforward book which examines the news-books and pamphlets produced during each general election in turn during Anne's reign. **286** looks at the collapse of censorship with the expiry of the Licensing Act of 1695, and at how Robert Harley created over the next twenty years a formidable set of government propaganda services. This is a far wider study than **285**, both conceptually and in terms of research. One episode which provided both official and free press with an opportunity, which they took, was the Junto's prosecution of a high Tory priest over an inflammatory sermon in 1709. The story – and its wide political and constitutional ramifications – are well told in **287**.

**288.** H. Horwitz, *Revolution politics* (1968)

**289.** A. MacInnes, *Robert Harley, tory politician* (1970)

**290.** H. T. Dickinson, *Bolingbroke* (1970)

**291.** S. Biddle, *Bolingbroke and Harley* (1975)

**292.** W. L. Sachse, *Lord Somers* (1975)

**293.** J. H. Plumb, *Sir Robert Walpole*, vol. 1 (1956)

**294.** J. Carswell, *The old cause* (1954)

The tories have found more and better biographers than have the Whigs. Horwitz offers an outstandingly clear and rounded portrait of the earl of Nottingham (**288**), MacInnes a brisk and sensible account of Harley (**289**), Dickinson a full and persuasive portrait of the enigmatic St John (**290**). **291** is an effective narrative account of the struggle for control of the Tory party in Anne's final years. In contrast, the only serious biography of a Whig leader in these years is **292**. Sachse is not helped by the fact that almost all Somers's papers were destroyed in a disastrous fire in 1758, but this is a dull life, better in accounting for particular episodes than for its overall assessment. The first 200 pages of Plumb's *Walpole* (**293**) are relevant and offer elegance and shrewdness of observation. **294** contains three character sketches, of which the First Lord Wharton comes into our period. Tory churchmen get better biographies than Whig ones too (see **497–8**). So it is all very unfair on the Whigs!

# 4
# POLITICAL AND CONSTITUTIONAL THOUGHT

It is not the intention of this chapter to enter into the realms of political science and philosophy. We are concerned with works of use to those studying history as history, and not with the discussion of ideas divorced from their historical context. Within this general area the last twenty years has seen the decline of one approach and the rise of another. The old-fashioned constitutional history which dominated the Oxford history school until the 1950s, and still is a viable tradition within that school today, looked at constitutional thought in terms of the distribution of power within the state and analysed debates about the nature of the government machine and the justifications offered for actions taken to control or change that machinery, treating such debates in relatively self-sufficient terms. Little effort was made, or thought given, to the social context within which institutions thrived, withered, evolved. The main thrust of this history was the consideration of statutes, proclamations and other formal acts, law reports, parliamentary speeches and petitions. Books, pamphlets and other published works were treated as largely subsidiary. Individuals were seen as spokesmen for particular causes, not as individual thinkers.

Work in the last twenty years has completely changed this emphasis. The minute study of statutes and legal judgments has given way to the analysis of political tracts, including ephemera, and to a concern with both the genealogy of ideas in a far wider sense (the relationship between political thought and wider social, cultural and religious movements, continental as well as English), with the social contexts within which men thought and wrote, and with the biographical context within which individual thinkers operated. The most important work of all along these lines has been initiated by Quentin Skinner, who has repeatedly urged that 'political texts must be understood according to their author's intentions and that these intentions can only be recognised by close attention to the linguistic conventions of the time' (this summary is by K. V. Thomas). Such an approach routs the exegetical approach of writers like Warrender who arrived at his view of Hobbes 'on the strength of reading *Leviathan* a number of times until its argument assumed some coherence'. One countervailing danger (though not in Skinner's own work) is that such an approach produces a species of historical writing insensitive to the practicalities of politics, and one which tends to give ideas an autonomy of rationalised self-interest that they do not possess; but it is generally to be welcomed. It is unfortunate, however, that the old approach has been jettisoned rather than adapted to take advantage of the new approaches. This chapter is divided into sections on themes and on the thought of particular individuals or groups. It will be found that the older tradition is to be found mainly in the former, the newer one in the latter.

**295.** D. L. Keir, *A constitutional history of modern Britain* (1934, 1969)

**296.** M. Thomson, *A constitutional history of England from 1642–1801* (1938)

**295** is the standard old-fashioned history, of which chapters 4 and 5 cover the seventeenth century. It is now in its ninth edition. **296** is written in a very dry, matter-of-fact tone, and tends to oversimplification, but it is admirably organised. Both are now largely superseded by the texts and comments in **28**.

**297.** C. Roberts, *The growth of responsible government in Stuart England* (1966)

**298.** A. H. Dodd, *The growth of responsible government* (1956)

**299.** C. C. Weston, *English constitutional theory and the House of Lords* (1965)

**297** is a major study of every aspect of the accountability of the governors to the governed and of the balance of power within the constitution, but is marred a little by its teleology. **298** traces the false starts as well as the steady development of effective legislative checks on royal executive freedom. Over half the book concerns the Stuart period. **299** offers an important study of the emergence of the idea of mixed monarchy in the early seventeenth century, and traces through succeeding decades the ideas laid out in the King's *Reply to the Nineteen Propositions*.

**300.** J. W. Gough, *Fundamental law in English history* (1955)

**301.** J. G. A. Pocock, *The ancient constitutions and the feudal law* (1957)

**302.** F. Thompson, *Magna Carta: its role in the making of the English constitution, 1300–1629* (1948)

**300** is a clear and sensible review of what seventeenth-century Englishmen meant by fundamental law and what British and American historians have taken them to mean. It is at its best on Sir Edward Coke and on James I and Charles I. **301** is 'a history of historiography' in the seventeenth century, tracing the emergence of a sense of development amongst English constitutionalist theories from Sir Henry Spelman onwards. **302** devotes almost half its space to the period 1603–29 and searches out the invocation of the charter by lawyers and parliamentarians.

**303.** W. H. Greenleaf, *Order, empiricism and politics* (1964)

**304.** D. Little, *Religion, order and law* (1971)

**305.** R. Eccleshall, *Order and reason in politics* (1964)

**303** chronicles the substitution of philosophical empiricism (as in Bacon, Harrington, Petty) for a static conception of order (as in James I, Forset, Filmer) as the organising principles of political thought. **304** examines that same concept of order in the puritan and anglican traditions of ecclesiastical and political thought and attempts thereby to recycle Weber's thesis of a link between protestanism and capitalism. **395** relates the concepts of reason and order to rival notices of absolute and limited monarchy. All three are 'difficult', over-schematic, and assume too easily genetic links between the minds of different thinkers.

**306.** J. W. Allen, *English political thought, 1603–60* vol. 1: *1603–44* (1940)

**307.** G. L. Mosse, *The struggle for sovereignty in England* (1950)

**308.** M. Judson, *The crisis of the constitution* (1949)

**309.** F. D. Wormuth, *The royal prerogative, 1603–1649* (1939)

**310.** P. Zagorin, *A history of political thought in the Puritan Revolution* (1966)

**306** was planned as the first of two volumes, but the second was never written. The thought of all the main and many subsidiary thinkers is clearly delineated, but the commentary is weak and the overall effect fragmentary. **307** sees the period from 1559 to 1629 as 'the age of competition for sovereignty', and rather unconvincingly finds the common lawyers unwittingly creating the case for a parliamentary absolutism. **308** more cogently argues that most constitutional thinking was sterile and half-baked until a civil war was unwittingly sprung upon the nation in 1642–3. **309** is a slender, pithy attempt to set the royal prerogative within its patriarchal setting. It is almost the only serious attempt to make sense of Arminian political theories. **310** is equally concise and energetic, and places the political thought of the radicals firmly into its theological context. It is a very clear and sensible introductory survey for all students. See also **A3**, **A7** (p. 179).

**311.** J. D. Eusden, *Puritans, lawyers and politics* (1958)

**312.** J. A. W. Gunn, *Politics and the public interest in the seventeenth century* (1969)

**313.** G. Schochet, *Patriarchalism in political thought* (1975)

**314.** C. B. MacPherson, *The political theory of possessive individualism* (1975)

These all attempt to relate political thought to a social context. **311** sets out to find puritans and common lawyers experiencing a common exclusion from power and a consequent kindred ideology. **312** is a 'political scientist's attempt at historical explanation' through the quest for the concept of an emergent 'public interest' in the political and economic tracts of the period 1640–1720. It does not convince. **313** looks at patriarchalism as a social reality in order to make more credible the widespread acclaim Filmer's platitudes received at the time. **314** is an impressive attempt to locate some unstated social assumptions in the work of Hobbes, Locke, Harrington and the Levellers, and to use this to unlock their thought. MacPherson's views on the Levellers have been seriously challenged (e.g. **42**, **193**, articles **X29**, **X46**) but he is agreeably harsh about Locke's thought.

**315.** W. K. Jordan, *Men of substance* (1942)

**316.** I. Coltman, *Private men and public causes* (1962)

**317.** M. Judson, *The political thought of Sir Henry Vane* (1960)

**315** contains the fullest account of the thought of Henry Parker, key apologist for parliament in 1642 and after. A fuller study is urgently needed. The account of Henry Robinson, advocate of religious toleration, free trade and a national bank, is also adequate rather than probing. **316** examines how men of integrity overcame their scruples and participated in the civil war. It concentrates on Hobbes, Sidney Godolphin, Ascham and the Great Tew circle. **317** is brief and lucid but makes Vane out to be more important and more comprehensible than he was (the judgement of Richard Baxter is more apposite: 'his unhappiness lay in this, that his doctrines were so cloudily formed and expressed that few could understand them and therefore he had but few true disciples').

**318.** F. Raab, *The English face of Macchiavelli* (1964)

**319.** J. G. A. Pocock, *The Macchiavellian moment* (1975)

**320.** Z. S. Fink, *The classical republicans* (1945)

**321.** J. H. M. Salmon, *The French wars of religion in English political thought* (1959)

**318** traces the impact of Macchiavelli on English thought. It is shrewd but flawed by an uncritical equation of Macchiavellianism with empiricism. **319** looks at the spread of the Florentine political thought throughout western Europe in the sixteenth and seventeenth centuries and beyond. It is more satisfactory than **318** but harder going. **319**, on the other hand, finds the oligarchical principles of Renaissance Venice as guiding the thought of Harrington, Milton, Neville and Sidney. **320** is able to be more precise and convincing about how much (and how late) the debates on sovereignty and contract in late-sixteenth-century France were taken up later in England.

**322.** F. H. Relf, *The Petition of Right* (1917)

**323.** C. Edie, *The Irish cattle bills* (1970)

These are straightforward accounts of the political and constitutional issues involved in attempts to restrain the royal prerogative. **322** still contains useful information, but the interpretative framework has been transformed by recent works such as **135** and **141** (also articles **X26–7**, **X59**, **X63**, **X176**). **323** is on a much less well-known subject, but an important one: it concerns a bill passed in 1666 which restrained the royal dispensing power.

**324.** S. Prall, *The agitation for law reform during the puritan revolution* (1966)

**325.** D. Veall, *The popular movement for law reform* (1970)

**324** is best at drawing attention to the ideas of neglected writers, and dealing with questions of sovereignty and with constitutional law as well as the villainy of lawyers. But it is fuzzy on political contexts. **325** concentrates more closely on the pamphlet literature (some 150 tracts in all) and shows how many of the causes taken up in the 1640s and 1650s had reached the statute book by 1700.

**326.** J. G. A. Pocock, *The political works of James Harrington* (1975)

**327.** C. Blitzer, *The political thought of James Harrington* (1960)

Harrington has undergone a great revival in recent times. **326** is a scholarly edition of his works with a learned if involved introduction. **327** is a sensible and clear introduction. See also **62**, **303**, **314**, **318**, **320**, **X205**.

**328.** D. D. Raphael, *Hobbes* (1977)

**329.** M. M. Goldsmith, *Hobbes' science of politics* (1970)

**330.** J. W. N. Watkins, *Hobbes' system of ideas* (1973)

**331.** H. Warrender, *The political philosophy of Hobbes* (1957)

**332.** K. C. Brown (ed.), *Hobbes studies* (1965)

**333.** J. Bowle, *Hobbes and his critics* (1951)

**334.** S. I. Mintz, *The hunting of Leviathan* (1962)

There is an immense literature on Hobbes, and the works listed are intended only as a cross-section of the various points of view and have been chosen mainly because of their clarity. **328** is a brief, clear introduction to Hobbes' political and ethical thought. It is probably better for the philosophy student than the historian. **329–32** offer a series of alternative approaches to his thought. **333** has little new to say about Hobbes, but offers useful accounts of the critiques of his thought by Filmer, Seth Ward, Lawson, Hunton and Clarendon. **334** is a more scholarly treatment of seventeenth-century reaction to Hobbes' materialism and determinism, concentrating on the free-will arguments of Cudworth and Bramhall.

**335.** M. Cranston, *John Locke: a biography* (1957)

**336.** R. Aaron, *John Locke* (3rd edition, 1971)

**337.** P. Laslett, *The two treatises on government* (1960)

**338.** J. Dunn, *The political thought of John Locke* (1969)

**339.** M. Seliger, *The liberal politics of John Locke* (1968)

**340.** J. W. Gough, *John Locke: political philosophy* (1950)

**341.** J. H. Franklin, *John Locke and the theory of sovereignty* (1978)

Locke's reputation amongst his contemporaries was far less notable or controversial than Hobbes'. He was not a pre-eminent political theorist. Yet his work bestrides modern scholarship to an even greater degree. Again, these seven works only scratch the surface. **335** is a very thoroughly researched and clearly presented life. **336** combines a brief biography with a thorough exposition of Locke's writings, particularly his theory of knowledge. **337** is an outstanding critical edition of his key political texts, which demolishes the view that Locke was the heir of Hobbes. **338** restores a religious dimension to Locke's thought. **339** reinterprets Locke's view of property in the light of the thought of Grotius and Pufendorf. **340** is a collection of eight lucid if lightweight essays. **341** seeks out the roots of Locke's notion of sovereignty. In the process it rehabilitates the thought of George Lawson, who wrote in the 1650s.

**342.** J. P. Kenyon, *Revolution principles* (1977)

**343.** H. T. Dickinson, *Liberty and property* (1977)

**344.** J. Hart, *Viscount Bolingbroke, tory humanist* (1965)

**345.** I. Kramnick, *Bolingbroke and his circle* (1968)

**342** is a very provocative and stimulating series of essays (based on the author's Ford Lectures at Oxford) which show how both Whig and Tory explanations of the Glorious Revolution develop and change in the decades that followed. It is mainly concerned with the Whigs. M. Goldie is producing a similar study of Tory thought. Only the first 120 pages of **343** cover our period. It too shows how Whig and Tory views change over time, but it also looks at court and country mentalities. It is less accurate and less probing than **342**. **344–5** are mainly concerned with Bolingbroke's toryism in the Walpolean era. **345** is the more readable and credible.

# 5

# MILITARY AND NAVAL AFFAIRS

Military and naval history are not growth subjects, except in one rather particular sense. In comparison with the scholarly interest in and indeed scholarly argument (even rancour) over modern warfare, interest in military history has flagged in recent decades. A romantic interest in antique weaponry, costume, etc. has led to the formation of societies such as the Sealed Knot which reenact civil-war engagements, and this in turn has bred interest in getting the details right, in establishing lines of march, numbers of men under arms, and so forth. Recent narrative histories of particular campaigns and the study of the strategy and tactics of particular generals or of the whole war are of a high order. But this has tended to turn military history into a distinct branch of history, and little attempt has been made to relate military change to social, economic or political history. The extent to which political or administrative considerations dictated the pattern of the English civil war remains obscure. Furthermore those few writers who address themselves to the bureaucracy of war approach it from a wider concern with civil government, and few have any expertise in matters of military technology. An important recent study by H. Tomlinson of the Ordnance Office under the later Stuarts might well establish a new trend, however. In view of the stress political historians have placed on the importance of the wars of 1689–1714 in transforming Britain's political and economic institutions, the lack of any work on the social history of those wars and the direct effect of recruitment, service and demobilisation of soldiers and sailors is very striking. The navy is much better served than the army in works spanning the century as a whole, but the above strictures about the narrow form of most of the works apply to the navy, if in an attenuated form. Certainly the recent appearance of **378** has helped. For other works with military themes see **111**, **172–3**, **178**, **180–2**, **210–15**, **267**, and articles **X54**, **X105**, **X108–9**, **X118**, **X127–8**, **X150–2**.

### The Army

**346.** P. Young and R. Holmes, *The English civil war* (1974)

**347.** A. Woolrych, *Battles of the English civil war* (1961)

**348.** R. Ollard, *This war without an enemy* (1976)

**349.** M. P. Ashley, *The English civil war: a concise history* (1974)

**350.** H. C. B. Rogers, *The English civil war* (1968)

**351.** R. Sherwood, *Civil strife in the Midlands* (1975)

**352.** J. Wroughton, *Civil war in Bath and north Somerset* (1973)

**346** is the fullest and clearest account of military operations during the civil war. It is less interested in logistics than with strategic planning and tactical manoeuvres, and (as a bashful non-military man) strikes me as emphasising minor engagements too much and sieges too little. Its handling of the political framework is far from flawless and some key articles on military operations have eluded the authors' sweep. **347** concentrates on key engagements but manages splendidly to place them in a wider military and political context. **348** and **349** are straightforward accounts and splendidly illustrated. **350** is a military man's alternative to **346**, much less successful than **346** as a narrative but is helpful in placing its maps of the engagements on modern ordnance surveys, allowing easy realisation for those who make field trips to battlefields (but beware of a misplacing of the royalist line at Naseby). **351** and **352** are awkwardly written but sound accounts of the campaigns and their effects on civilian life in the Midlands and the area around Bath.

**353.** P. Young, *Edgehill, 1642* (1967)

**354.** P. Young, *Marston Moor, 1644* (1970)

**355.** P. Wenham, *The great and close siege of York, 1644* (1970)

**356.** J. Adair, *Cheriton, 1644* (1974)

**357.** M. Toynbee and P. Young, *Cropredy Bridge, 1644* (1970)

**358.** P. Young and W. Embleton, *Sieges of the great civil war* (1979)

A series of studies produced by the Roundwood Press, each dealing with one civil war campaign. **353** has a long and useful introduction on the English soldiery of 1642 and examines recruitment, pay and conditions on both sides. It then looks at the campaign and at the battle itself in detail. Like all six studies, it has extensive appendices printing original documents, including accounts of the battle as seen from both sides. **354** is similar to **353** in all respects, but **355–8** are more exclusively concerned with the campaigns themselves, though **355** gives extensive quotations from the York Corporation manuscripts. **358** helps to redress an imbalance in the literature, and is very well done, although more space might have been devoted to the technology and military expertise of siegecraft, and less to case studies.

**359.** M. Ashley, *Rupert of the Rhine* (1976)

**360.** P. Morrah, *Prince Rupert of the Rhine* (1976)

**361.** F. T. R. Edgar, *Sir Ralph Hopton, the king's man in the west* (1968)

**362.** J. Adair, *Roundhead General: A military biography of Sir William Waller* (1976)

**363.** P. Young, *Oliver Cromwell* (1962)

**364.** J. Gillingham, *Cromwell: portrait of a soldier* (1976)

**365.** H. G. Tibbutt, *Colonel John Okey, 1606–1662* (1955)

**366.** M. Ashley, *Cromwell's generals* (1954)

Most of these biographies describe their heroes but fail to explain them, and few illuminate the age rather than the man. **360**, however, is a scholarly and sympathetic view of Rupert, and **366** is one of Ashley's best books. It examines all the leading figures in the army between 1649 and 1660, attempting to merge a narrative of the decade with the career of each in turn (Fairfax, Ireton, Harrison, Lambert, etc.) as each became dominant. There is a useful chapter on the major-generals in their provincial cantons (1655–7) and an account of the Scottish campaigns of 1650–2.

**367.** C. H. Firth, *Cromwell's army* (1902, 1962)

**368.** C. H. Firth and G. Davies, *A regimental history of Cromwell's army* (2 vols., 1940)

**369.** P. Young and W. Embleton, *The cavalier army* (1976)

**370.** I. Roy (ed.), *The royalist Ordnance papers* (2 vols., 1965, 1975)

**367** is a classic, a rounded and convincing portrait of an extraordinary army, its structure, discipline, commissariat, etc. The chapters on religion and politics are still fundamental to any understanding of the army. Work in progress by M. Kishlansky, H. Reece and others will modify this picture, but the book's value and readability will remain. **368** is a two-volume source book for the *cognoscenti*. The royalist army is poorly served (not least for evidential reasons). **369** will meet the needs of enthusiastic amateurs, but the introductory essays in **370** (published by the Oxford Record Society) must suffice for the moment as appetizers for the major work I. Roy has in hand.

**371.** J. Childs, *The army of Charles II* (1976)

**372.** H. Tomlinson, *Guns and government* (1979)

**371** is a solid, sensible work with too many minor inaccuracies for comfort, but it shows why contemporaries believed that the army of Charles had increased, was increasing and ought to be diminished. It was small but it did exist. A second volume on the army under James II is to be published. **372** is a careful and thorough study of the Ordnance Office in the period 1660–1714. It examines the personnel, business and efficiency of this important back-up to the army and navy at a time of escalating and expensive warfare. There is an excellent chapter on the relationship between the Ordnance Office and the other agencies of central government (council – and its committees – secretaries of state, admiralty, etc.).

**373.** R. E. Scouller, *The armies of Queen Anne* (1966)

**374.** C. Barnett, *Marlborough* (1976)

**375.** D. Chandler, *Marlborough as military commander* (1979)

**376.** D. Chandler, *The art of warfare in the age of Marlborough* (1976)

**373** is a thorough and scholarly analysis by a military man of the organisation and administration of Marlborough's army. It deals with recruitment, pay, quartering, supplies, etc. There is an outstanding chapter on discipline and morale. **374** is easily the best of the popular biographies of Marlborough and brings out his neurosis and complexity of character. It has a wealth of illustrations. **375** is fuller, with excellent maps, but is too narrowly concerned with the fighting. It can safely be described as adulatory. **376** is more balanced, and is an excellent popular study with splendid illustrations.

## The Navy

**377.** M. Lewis, *The history of the British Navy* (1957)

**378.** P. M. Kennedy, *The rise and fall of British naval supremacy* (1976)

**379.** R. G. Albion, *Forests and sea power* (1926)

**380.** H. W. Richmond, *The navy as an instrument of policy, 1558–1727* (1953)

**381.** J. S. Corbett, *England and the Mediterranean, 1603–1713* (2 vols., 1904)

**377** is an old and very general Penguin history, largely superseded by **378**, an impressive account of the relationship between sea power and the resources and demands of the British economy. Only the first eighty pages are relevant, but they are clear and well-informed. One aspect of this problem is treated by **379** mainly for the period after 1700, but important on England's diminishing woodlands and the switch of supply from the Baltic to America. **380** concentrates on the debate amongst English politicians of the 'Blue Water' and 'Continental' schools about military and naval priorities in war and peace. It also emphasises the intricate relationship between naval strategy and trade patterns. **381** is a well-sustained narrative of 'the rise and influence of British power within the straits'. It treats the subject strictly chronologically, but successfully relates naval to diplomatic and military affairs. It is weak, however, on the relationship between naval activity and commercial interests.

**382.** M. Oppenheim, *A history of the administration of the royal navy, 1509–1660* (1913)

**383.** C. D. Penn, *The navy under the early Stuarts* (1913)

**384.** J. R. Powell, *The navy in the English civil war* (1962)

**385.** A. W. Tedder, *The navy of the restoration* (1916)

**382** is written like a textbook, with marginal paragraph heads, and it is quite narrow in its focus. But it still provides accurate information about naval administration, about pay and conditions and about the distinctions between, and the overlapping of, royal and merchant shipping. **383** offers a chronological survey of the period 1603–49, and is still useful on the naval chaos of 1614–19 and on the 'ship money' fleets of the 1630s, but it has been supplanted on the 1620s and the 1640s. **384** is a fair assessment of the importance of the navy in parliament's victory over the king. It is clearly written and not overstated. **385** is a complement to **383**. It covers the years 1658–67 and gives an excellent account of the course of the Second Dutch War. But its chapters on administration are rendered redundant by **391–3**.

**386.** E. B. Powley, *The navy in the revolution of 1688* (1928)

**387.** G. N. Clark, *The Dutch alliance and the war against French trade, 1688–1697* (1923)

**388.** J. Ehrman, *The navy in the wars of William III* (1953)

**389.** F. P. Aubrey, *The defeat of James Stuart's armada, 1692* (1979)

**390.** J. H. Owen, *The war at sea under Queen Anne* (1933)

**386** looks in detail at the period November 1688 to June 1690. It contains an important study of James II's campaign in Ireland and of the siege of Londonderry. **387** was Clark's first book and it offers a clear account of the problems of trading with enemies and neutrals. Its chapters on privateering are now redundant, but it is still useful otherwise. **388** is a vast and detailed work. The first part analyses the ships, materials and supplies, dockyards, officers and men, victuals and estimates and accounts. The second gives an account of the war in progress from 1688 to 1698. **389** is a narrative account of the naval actions at Barfleur and La Hogue which disrupted Louis XIV's plans to invade England and reimpose James II. Similarly, **390** offers a narrative of the engagements and the defence of merchantmen between 1702 and 1708. It contains a brief introductory chapter on the size and organisation of the navies.

**391.** R. Ollard, *Pepys* (1976)

**392.** Sir A. Bryant, *Pepys* (3 vols., 1933–8)

**393.** R. Ollard, *Man of war: Sir Richard Holmes and the Restoration navy* (1969)

**391** is a straightforward, unaffected biography. **392** is a long, detailed work strongest on Pepys's work at the admiralty. **393** is a more recent and scholarly appreciation of the achievements of the Restoration. Those interested in Pepys will, however, bypass the above and go straight to the magnificent edition of his diary edited in nine volumes by R. C. Latham and W. Matthews. Pepys's administrative papers are to be edited for the Naval Record Society by H. Tomlinson over the next few years.

# 6
# ECCLESIASTICAL HISTORY

In many ways, our understanding of seventeenth-century ecclesiastical history is better than our understanding of most other aspects of the period. The history of those religious groups – protestant and catholic – who dissented from the Church of England has been well established, particularly impressive work having been done on the sociology of their beliefs. The major developments in theological thought have been identified and discussed. The fragmentation of the Calvinist–protestant consensus, especially in the 1640s, has been exhaustively discussed. Enough bishops left enough papers and have found enough biographers for us to have a clear impression of the aspirations, integrity and achievements of the leaders of the church.

All, however, is not well. The year 1660 stands as a great divide here as in political history. There are very few books which span the whole period, and none which treat broad issues throughout the period. Such general works as do exist tackle the period from the Reformation or from 1559 down to 1660. It is very difficult indeed to discover in what sense the Restoration church was a return to the church of Elizabeth and James I or the church of Charles I and Laud. Indeed, there is very little writing on the anglican church as a church in the early part of the century. In the 1640s men fought expressly and purposefully to defend 'the true reformed protestant church as by law established' and the Book of Common Prayer. They were believing, practising *anglicans*. Yet our books are concerned overwhelmingly with those who rejected the church or sought to reform it. The man in the pew, the 'silent majority' of ordinary Christians have had a very raw deal. Indeed, the history of the church in the seventeenth century has consisted largely of the history of ecclesiastics, theologians and dissidents. Although some have written about the 'godly gentleman' we know more about the archetype than about actual examples.

One way this problem could be overcome is by more local studies. Our understanding of the Elizabethan church has been transformed by such works as C. Haigh's *Reformation and resistance in Tudor Lancashire* or R. B. Manning's *Religion and society in Elizabethan Sussex*. But there is no comparable work on the early seventeenth century. Very recently a pioneering study has appeared on the parish clergy of Leicestershire in the late seventeenth century, and this is an encouraging sign, but it was a group biography not an analysis of clerical functions or aspirations. Several extremely important Ph.D. theses are expected to be published during the next few years. They will fill enormous gaps and should inspire revisions of other accepted views. These include N. R. N. Tyacke's work on the Laudians, M. Ingram's study of the institutions of Christian marriage and of sexual misconduct as revealed by the ecclesiastical records of Wiltshire, and R. Beddard's study of the archiepiscopate of William Sancroft. Once these have appeared, the most glaring weaknesses will be a modern appraisal of the Jacobean church and an analysis of the decline of apocolyptic beliefs in the late seventeenth century.

The subdivisions in most of the chapters of this book selected themselves. The early chapters fell naturally into chronological subdivisions; the social and economic chapters equally naturally fell into topical divisions. This was the only difficult chapter to arrange. As I said, the year 1660 stands as a fundamental historiographical divide, but it is the only one. On the other hand, most of the books deal firmly with either anglicans, puritans, the separatists or the Roman Catholics, and this ultimately seemed the clearest set of criteria to use. To distinguish anglicans from puritans cuts across my own view of things and the trend of recent scholarship, but it is unquestionably the way history has been written up in the past.

## General Works

**394.** H. G. Alexander, *Religion in England, 1558–1662* (1968)

**395.** C. Cross, *Church and people, 1450–1660* (1976)

**396.** W. K. Jordan, *The rise of toleration*, vol. 2: *1603–40*, and vols. 3 & 4: *1640–1660* (1932–40)

**397.** W. Lamont, *Godly rule* (1969)

**398.** G. R. Cragg, *From puritanism to the age of reason* (1966)

**399.** G. Nuttall and O. Chadwick (eds.), *From uniformity to unity* (1962)

**400.** N. Sykes, *Old priest and new presbyter* (1956)

**394** is a very straightforward and effective introduction. Over half the book is devoted to the period 1603–62, and the main developments in ecclesiastical policy and in theology are discussed. It is weak on what was happening at a parish level and is running out of steam by the 1640s, but it can be recommended to school and college students. It also contains excellent bibliographies. **395** is more ambitious but is not altogether successful. In 240 pages it attempts to review the impact of the Reformation on English society and institutions. Its subtitle is *The triumph of the laity in the English church* but most of the users I have discussed it with find it overschematic, particularly in the final chapters. On Laud, for example, it is better to begin with the relevant chapter in **150**. **396** is an immensely long and frankly tedious exposition of the rise of a theory of religious toleration. There are endless problems of perspective, particularly the assumed link between religious freedom and political liberalism and the unconvincing notion that by 1660 'responsible opinion' was persuaded of the virtue of religious freedom. So it is at best a source-book to be plundered. By contrast, **397** is a pithy, argumentative book which shows how far both the puritans and their establishment opponents looked forward to the millenium. It also claims to find a reaction against high eschatologies in the erastian rebellion of the 1640s. Lamont probably conflates different streams of eschatological thought, but he has certainly written a stimulating book. **398** tells a very different story, the triumph of reason, of pietism, of latitudinarianism in the late seventeenth century. It prompts an unanswered question: whatever happened to Zeal? **399** is a collection of eight essays to commemorate the tercentenary of the Act of Uniformity. There are four central to our period: A. Whiteman offers a moderate and irenical review of the ecclesiastical settlement itself; E. Ratcliff considers the Savoy Conference of 1661 and the reformed prayer book of 1662; G. Nuttall discusses the mentality of the early non-conformists; and R. Thomas looks at the political and theological arguments which drew some men between 1662 and 1689 to urge a more comprehensive church, others to urge greater toleration outside the church, and most to refute both. **400** examines Anglican doctrines of the church and the priesthood since the Reformation; the seventeenth-century chapters are lucid and cover ground not treated anywhere else.

**401.** E. Rose, *Cases of conscience* (1974)

This is a witty and nicely judged book which looks at the way men of integrity not cut out for martyrdom coped with issues of conscience. In other words, it compares the ways those catholics and puritans who wished to accept the secular power of the crown and to live peaceably under it without submitting to the full commands of royal and episcopal supremacy lived with their consciences and the law. It is much thinner, unfortunately, on James I's reign than on Elizabeth's.

**402.** R. B. Knox (ed.), *Reformation conformity and dissent* (1977)

This is a *Festschrift* for G. Nuttall, and includes a number of seventeenth-century contributions of wide interest. The editor writes on bishops in the pulpit, G. Rupp on 'a devotion to rapture in English puritanism', B. White on Henry Jessey (whom he shows to have been more than a marginal Baptist figure), C. Hill writes on occasional conformity, R. Tudur Jones on Welsh puritan pietism, B. Hall on Daniel Defoe and Scotland. There is a suggestive general article by R. L. Greaves on 'the nature of the puritan tradition'. All in all this is one of the most satisfying of the recent *Festschriften* (and one of the most reasonably priced!)

### The Church of England

**403.** H. R. McAdoo, *The spirit of anglicanism* (1965)

**404.** G. O. Addleshaw, *The high church tradition* (1941)

**405.** G. O. Addleshaw and F. Etchells, *The architectural setting of anglican worship* (1948)

**406.** H. Davies, *Worship and theology in England*, vol. II: *from Andrews to Baxter and Fox (1603–1690)* (1975)

**407.** J. R. Phillips, *The reformation of the images* (1973)

**403** offers a detailed exposition of the thought of a number of influential anglican thinkers – Hooker, Hales, Chillingworth, the Arminians, the Latitudinarians. These men are made to represent the anglican tradition by default (there is little mention here of Perkins, Sibbes, Preston or any other of those 'puritans' who saw themselves as anglicans at least down to the 1640s). The book is further flawed by the narrow range of topics explored (ones more obviously of interest to modern theologians than the anti-papal and eschatological writings central to seventeenth-century concern). Two pairs of chapters on the new scientific movement and on the appeal to antiquity are much weaker. On what the author does talk about, however, anglican 'theological method', this book is excellent. **404** is exclusively concerned with the defence of the Book of

Common Prayer in the seventeenth century, while **405** covers the whole of the period since the Reformation but contains an important chapter on Laudian principles of church architecture. **406** is a far longer, far broader, far duller book, often repetitive and prolix. It is, however, authoritative and immensely well-researched. The first two hundred pages discuss the context of worship, church architecture, spiritual exercises propounded by devotional literature as preparation for worship, and the role of sermons as a 'stimulus to worship'. The next hundred pages look at Roman, Arminian and puritan styles of worship – attitudes to music, to the Christian calendar, to the status of the sacrament of Holy Communion. The final part examines liturgical formularies and their use – the Book of Common Prayer, the Directory of Public Worship, the forms used by Baptists, etc. **407** is concerned with the destruction of art in England in the period 1535–1660 and is predominantly on the restoration of church art by Laud and the new wave of iconoclasm in the mid-seventeenth century.

**408.** R. Marchant, *The church under the law* (1969)

**409.** R. Marchant, *Puritans and the church courts in the Diocese of York* (1960)

**410.** R. Usher, *The rise and fall of High Commission* (1913, 1968)

**411.** R. E. Head, *Royal supremacy and the trial of bishops, 1558–1725* (1962)

One aspect of religious life little changed at the Reformation was ecclesiastical justice. The same anomalous structure of courts and jurisdictions retained control over the enforcement of eight of the ten commandments (the state had taken over the sixth and eighth). It has been generally held that they became increasingly ineffective. In **408–9** a more qualified judgement is accorded. Both books deal with the bishopric of York and its subsidiary jurisdictions (archdeacons, rural deans, etc.) and with the archdeaconry of Nottingham (1560–1640). They argue that the courts were cheaper, quicker and in general less corrupt than the lay courts, and Marchant also finds evidence of a more irenical intention in Elizabethan and Jacobean bishops than has usually been acknowledged. The coming of Archbishop Neile is seen as a great turning point. **408** is concerned with the general work of the courts, particularly the enforcement of norms of social and sexual conduct, the management of church finances and the handling of testamentory affairs, while **409** is about the enforcement of religious uniformity.

Both make hard but worthwhile reading. A very important book on the church's regulations of marriage and sexual misconduct in Wiltshire, 1580–1640, by M. Ingram, will be published shortly. Above the diocesan courts stood the Court of High Commission, the only church court with teeth. **410** is an elderly and serviceable account of its rise and fall, recently reprinted with an important introductory essay by Tyler to bring it up to date and relate the northern High Commission to the southern one. **411** attempts to discover how the crown used its authority over the bishops. It has good accounts of the trials of Abbot, Williams and Goodman in the early seventeenth century and of Scottish bishops after the Restoration: a useful if derivative work.

**412.** C. Hill, *The economic problems of the church* (1956)

**413.** P. Hembry, *The bishops of Bath and Wells, 1540–1640* (1967)

**414.** R. O'Day and F. Heal (eds.), *Continuity and change* (1976)

**415.** R. O'Day, *The English clergy: the emergence and consolidation of a profession, 1558–1642* (1979)

**412** is one of Hill's best books. It looks at the impoverishment of the church and of churchmen in an age of plunder and inflation, and at the attempts of Laud to restore the autonomy of the church. Although recent work has suggested that the picture is overdrawn the central thesis is compelling, and a subject which could have been one of the dullest to read about is brought to life. It covers the period 1580 to 1640. **413** is a case study in the way crown and courts plundered the living bishops, and the bishops themselves plundered their heirs. It is a sordid tale clearly and readably told, and the Jacobean and Caroline periods emerge more honourably than they do in other respects. **414** is a collection of essays derived from a colloquium held at Cambridge concerning the Reformation in its local setting. It must be said that most of the essays make dull reading, but those concerned wholly or in part with the Stuarts are amongst the liveliest. See, in particular, R. O'Day's chapter on the education of the clergy, 1560–1640, R. Houlbrooke on the decline of the church courts, and R. Foster on the work of Archbishop Neile of York. **415** is a major new study of the 'professionalisation' of the clergy and looks at recruitment, education, living standards and efficacy as well as offering an immensely thorough study of patronage.

**416.** R. Usher, *The reconstruction of the Church of England* (2 vols., 1910)

**417.** R. Babbage, *Puritanism and Richard Bancroft* (1964)

**418.** H. R. McAdoo, *The structure of Caroline moral theology* (1949)

**419.** C. E. Bourne, *The anglicanism of Archbishop Laud* (1947)

**420.** R. Orr, *Reason and authority: the thought of William Chillingworth* (1967)

**421.** G. R. Cragg, *Freedom and authority* (1974)

**416** is basic and venerable. It is over 800 pages long and is concerned exclusively with the years 1603–10. It falls into three parts: the first looks at the state of the church in 1603; the second examines the abortive reforming conference at Hampton Court in 1603 and at the fundamental codification represented by the Canons of Convocation of 1604. The third section concerns the debate on those canons in parliament and elsewhere and at the enforcement of the settlement on recusants and puritans. What it says about Hampton Court and the deprivations is redundant (see article **X234**), but the section on the canons is still basic. **417** is a very specific study of Bancroft's attempts to enforce those canons. It is conceived too narrowly from a clerical point of view, and many would find its assumption that Bancroft was fighting a heroic rear-guard action against the advance of puritanism much too teleological. But it is an important study. **418** is an early pilot scheme for **402**, and is a study of the moral theology of a small group of thinkers – above all Hooker, Sanderson and Jeremy Taylor. It is concerned with several issues – conscience and the law, mortal and venial sin, repentance and holiness. **419** was welcomed by Norman Sykes with the words 'Archbishop Laud has suffered as much at the hands of historians as Job at those of his friends'. This is very much a work of special pleading, an openly polemical defence of Laud as theologian and statesman. It should be read, but only when a basic grasp of his life and failure have been gleaned from **483**. **420** is a more important account of a lesser man. Chillingworth converted to Rome in 1628 and back in 1637, becoming an important member of the Great Tew Circle. He sought both to sanction the power of human reason and to acknowledge the authority of the institutional church. This led him to plead for the reunification of Christendom. It is an important study of a man whose personal struggle crystallised some of the greatest intellectual tensions in the seventeenth century. **421** looks at such problems in that broader sense. It argues that 'the early part of the seventeenth century attempted to define the basis of freedom and its legitimate extent but found that preoccupation with authority restricted the claims that could usefully be advanced'. I felt uneasy with the definition of liberty and found the whole book difficult and technical, but its scope is very broad – Hooker, Andrewes, the puritans, the separatists and the recusants. It covers the years 1603–40.

**422.** W. A. Shaw, *A history of the English church during the civil wars and under the commonwealth* (2 vols., 1900)

**423.** S. W. Carruthers, *Everyday work of the Westminster Assembly* (1943)

**424.** J. W. Packer, *The transformation of anglicanism, 1643–1660* (1969)

**422** is what you would expect from the man who had spent the previous twenty years calendaring the Treasury Books. It is learned, dull and overwhelmingly concerned with bureaucracy. It falls into four parts: 'the ecclesiastical debates of the Long Parliament' (1640–3); the work of the Westminster Assembly (1643–7); the presbyterian system (1646–60); and patronage and financial problems. It remains fundamental and only part 3 has been really revised by modern work. **423** is, as its title implies, a chronicle of the affairs of the assembly in its early active years of 1643–7. It is mercifully brief. **424** looks at how the Church of England accommodated to the trauma of extinction, and does so through an analysis of the writings of Henry Hammond. It finds a transmogrified Laudian theology ready for the task in hand in 1660.

**425.** R. S. Bosher, *The making of the Restoration settlement* (1951)

**426.** G. R. Abernathy, *The English presbyterians and the Stuart restoration, 1649–1663* (1965)

**427.** I. M. Green, *The re-establishment of the church of England, 1660–1663* (1978)

How a narrow and intransigent anglicanism came to be re-imposed by parliament at the Restoration is one of the most puzzling problems in the whole period. These three books present widely divergent and compelling interpretations. **425** argues that the final settlement was the one always sought by Clarendon and his 'Laudian' allies, and that the comprehension schemes of 1660–1 were at best disingenuous and at worst two-faced. **426** lays the responsibility on the political and religious presbyterians who were divided, indecisive and intransigent over the wrong issues at the wrong moments.

Its critique of **425** is effective but it fails to offer a convincing definition of 'presbyterianism' in the context of 1660. **427** argues for a gradual change of attitude by Charles and Clarendon and for a greater clash of aims than the others have allowed. It too is at its most effective in undermining **425**, and on establishing what happened at a local level, but it presumes too much foreknowledge to be an introductory guide. Use it alongside the chapters by Whiteman and Ratcliff in **399**. Wormald's discussion of Clarendon's religious ideas in **163** is also highly pertinent.

**428.** N. Sykes, *From Sheldon to Secker* (1959)

**429.** W. G. Simon, *The Restoration episcopate* (1965)

**430.** J. H. Pruett, *The parish clergy under the later Stuarts: the Leicestershire experience* (1978)

**431.** C. J. Sommerville, *Popular religion in Restoration England* (1977)

**428** is a brilliant set of Ford Lectures in Oxford which explains why the Church of England failed to overhaul the church courts, finances or worship in the century after 1660 despite some able and committed reforming bishops. **429** is simply a weak group biography. **430** is a very thorough analysis of the geographical and educational and social background of Leicestershire parsons, and of their wealth and authority. By leaving curates out of account it draws too optimistic a conclusion, but it is a useful and pleasantly written piece. The title of **431** is a rather unhelpful one. It is an examination of the beliefs and attitudes expressed into religious 'best-sellers' of the period. It is interesting in its discussion of the reading public and of cheap religious publishing, but the statistical method used to describe the theological content of the works is unsatisfying.

**432.** G. Every, *The high church party, 1688–1718* (1956)

**433.** G. Straka, *Anglican reactions to the revolution of 1688* (1968)

**434.** J. Redwood, *Reason, ridicule and religion* (1976)

**435.** N. Sykes, *Church and State in the eighteenth century* (1934)

**432** is short, difficult and worthwhile. Its view of politics is naive and outdated, but it is excellent both in its discussion of the great debates of the time within the church – comprehension, convocation, occasional conformity, the non-juring schism – and also in discovering a distinctive theological tradition which was forming in the pre-1688 church and which came to fruition in the reign of

Anne. **433** studies the writings of anglican divines and is intent on showing why so few became non-jurors. Most are shown to have clung to a 'providentialist' theory of the events of 1688. **434** is an intelligent but chronically inaccurate book which got reviewers vying to compile the longest list of factual errors. It could have been called 'the secularisation of the English mind in the late seventeenth century'. It traces a linear development from religion to rationalism and deism which is oversimplified conceptually and tends to conflate anticlericalism and secularism. **435** covers the period from 1660 and examines the role of the church theoretically rather than chronologically (e.g. the role of the bishops in the House of Lords, the office and functions of bishops within the diocese, the political nature of ecclesiastical preferments, etc.). An authoritative and elegantly written book.

### The Puritan Tradition

**436.** M. M. Reese, *The puritan impulse, 1559–1660* (1975)

**437.** W. Haller, *The rise of puritanism* (1938)

**438.** W. Haller, *Liberty and reformation in the puritan revolution* (1955)

**439.** J. H. F. New, *Puritan and anglican* (1964)

**440.** J. S. M. McGee, *The godly man in Stuart England* (1976)

**441.** C. H. and K. George, *The protestant mind of the English Reformation, 1570–1640* (1961)

**442.** C. Hill, *Society and puritanism in pre-revolutionary England* (1966)

**443.** C. Hill, *The intellectual origins of the English Revolution* (1963)

**436** is an introductory survey to the political role of puritanism and is intended for students. The opening chapter on the nature of puritanism is stimulating and lively, but the author tries to fit too much into a hundred pages and the book tails off badly in the sections on the period after 1603. **437** is a classic, based on a systematic explication of the writings of 'puritan' divines. But it assumes a linear development and an inexorable 'rise'. **438** takes up the story in 1642 and continues it to 1649. Again it is based on sermons, pamphlets and tracts and becomes riveted by the quest for the freedom enjoyed by modern liberal democracies rather than seventeenth-century Englishmen. The strictly chronological approach also makes the developments hard to follow. **439–40** are dubious attempts to establish distinctive anglican and puritan theologies. **439** is brisk and incisive, analysing the ideas of two clusters of writers on doctrines of the Fall, nature and grace, scripture, the church, the sacraments, eschatology and ethics. **440** is a longer, more plodding book which centres on writings about 'man's duties towards God and his neighbours'. By lumping 'those who protested against the rise of Arminianism' into his puritan group, McGee makes both the archbishops and a majority of the bishops of the 1620s into puritans. But both it and **439** fall into a deeper error of assuming too clear and linear an intellectual and ecclesiological tradition from 1560 to 1640 and beyond. **441** refuses to find a puritan–anglican polarity but falls into the opposite trap of failing to locate a spectrum and assuming too great a uniformity. This however is a venial sin. There are excellent chapters on the political thought of churchmen, on protestant ideas about the family, sex and Christianity, and a sensible critique of the Weber–Tawney thesis of a relationship between capitalism and protestantism. **442–3** are highly characteristic works. **442** explains what it is about the changing economics and social conditions in England in the century before 1640 that made the spread of radical protestant ideas probable and shaped them in new ways. It has, quite rightly, been a most influential work. **443**, on the other hand, has commanded far less support, though the central thesis, which finds a relationship between puritanism and progressive ideas about the law and science, has generated a lively debate (see **42**).

**444.** B. W. Ball, *A great expectation* (1975)

**445.** C. Hill, *Antichrist in the seventeenth century* (1971)

**446.** P. Christianson, *Reformers and Babylon* (1978)

**447.** K. Firth, *The apocolyptic tradition in Reformation Britain, 1530–1645* (1978)

Millenarianism is one of the most thoroughly worked-out themes of recent years (see **397, 402, 458, 465, 503**). **444** is the most theologically sophisticated. Ball establishes a broad context by examining the doctrine of Christ's second coming, interpretations of the books of Daniel and Revelation, and attitudes to prophecy throughout the Reformation period, before homing in on seventeenth-century England and finding that 'it was still possible to believe in the Fifth Monarchy without being fanatical, to be a millenarian without believing in the Fifth Monarchy, and to expect the imminent second coming without being a millenarian at all'. **445** is an important study of the shift of focus within English writings on the antichrist. Puritans came to see antichrist not so much in the person of the Pope as in the stain of sin in every man. This sinfulness was borne out in the flaws in the existing church. This in turn had a liberating effect for those intent on building a New Jerusalem after the civil war. **446** is a detailed analysis of the writings of a large number of divines and looks at the increasingly distinct traditions of apocalyptic thought. The most generally useful section is probably the last, on the calls for a New Jerusalem in 1640–2. **447** is more narrowly concerned with an intellectual tradition working its way through a relatively small number of authors from Bale to Hartlib and Comenius via Foxe and William Hakewill. **445–6** are for the less expert, **444**, **447** for the specialist.

**448.** H. Davies, *The worship of the English puritans* (1948)

**449.** R. C. Greaves, *The puritan revolution in educational thought* (1969)

**450.** O. C. Watkins, *The puritan experience* (1972)

**448** is a wide-ranging work that deals not only with the mainstream 'presbyterian' tradition but also with the separatists, and looks at the proposed service-books, at sacramental theology, at preaching, at catechising, and at music and art in puritan worship. On preaching it has been overtaken by more recent books (e.g. **452**), and the central argument has been subsumed into the author's later work (**406**), but this book retains an independent value. It also has an unfussy and sensible way of defining puritanism. **449** shows that the debates over a new model for the church in the mid-seventeenth century spilled over into a full-scale debate over the ends and means of education. **450** is a straightforward and thoughtful account of two hundred and more spiritual autobiographies written before 1725.

**451.** R. C. Richardson, *Puritanism in north-west England* (1972)

**452.** P. Seaver, *The puritan lectureships, 1560–1662* (1970)

**451** assumes too readily that puritans can be apprehended, put in a card-index and processed there, but there is much provocative material in this book, both about the increasing importance of lay puritanism and about the struggle for control in particular parishes in the diocese of Chester. The book covers the period 1570–1640.

The first third of **452** looks at the establishment of lectureships throughout England and at the struggle between local authorities and the crown and the bishops to control them. The main body of the book examines the London lectureships, their number, location and purpose, the careers of the lecturers, and the ineffectiveness of succesive bishops. It is an important study, though it assumes too great a uniformity in the meaning of the term 'lecturer'.

### The separatists

**453.** M. R. Watts, *The dissenters* (vol. 1, 1977)

The first 350 pages cover the period down to 1720. It is arguably over-schematic and tends to ignore theological complexities, but it is an epic venture and an excellent introductory survey which clearly delineates all the main trends.

**454.** B. R. White, *The English separatist tradition* (1971)

**455.** M. Tolmie, *The triumph of the saints* (1977)

**454** covers the period 1553–1620 and is excellent where so many other books are weak, in establishing the theological differences between the leaders without invoking denominational labels inappositely or anachronistically. A crisp, clear book. **455** takes over with the establishment of Henry Jacob's church in London in 1616 and traces the history of the particular and general baptist churches in the capital down to 1649. The book contains a very important section on the organisational links between the Baptists and the Levellers.

**456.** G. Nuttall, *Visible saints* (1957)

**457.** G. Yule, *The independents in the English civil war* (1958)

**458.** J. F. Wilson, *Pulpit in parliament* (1969)

**456** is a study of the congregational churches in the period 1640–60 based around four key principles: separation, fellowship, freedom and fitness (to be called). It is challenging and shrewd, but it is occasionally blurred chronologically and the syntax is often awkward. **457** is far less successful in its attempt to show a close relationship between political 'independents' and religious 'independents' in the late 1640s. It falls into a large number of traps of nomenclature and definition. **458** examines the Fast sermons in the Long Parliament and argues that the differences between presbyterians and independents appear more clearly in the heightened eschatology of the latter than in the shaded differences of ecclesiology. Not an easy book to read, but the straightforward early chapters on the political 'uses' of the sermons and on the patronage of particular preachers are worth reading on their own.

**459.** H. Maclachan, *Socinianism in the seventeenth century* (1951)

**460.** G. Huehns, *Antinomianism in English history* (1961)

**461.** D. P. Walker, *The decline of hell* (1964)

Socinianism is a heresy which denies the deity and atoning sacrifice of Christ. **459** sees its spread in England from 1640 to 1700 as one manifestation of the rational, sceptical mood emerging at that time. There were no Socinian sects as such, but an increasing number of people within the separatist churches abandoned Trinitarian belief and moving to Socinian or kindred heresies. The book gives an excellent account of John Biddle and his persecution in the Protectorate. **460** concentrates its attention on the period 1640–60 and considers those who believed that 'the moral law is not binding upon Christians under the law of Grace'. It is clear but cautious in applying the label of Levellers and Fifth Monarchists and in finding it at work amongst the Quakers. **461** is, perhaps, a work of theology rather than history, but it includes a concise discussion of '17th century discussions of eternal torment'. The first part looks in general at the strengths and weaknesses of the doctrine, the second part at Socinian, Arian and Platonist challenges to it from the mid-century, and the rise of the theodicy and the Philadelphians later.

**462.** C. Hill, *The world turned upside down (1972)*

**463.** C. Hill, *Gerrard Winstanley: the law of freedom and other writings* (1973)

**464.** C. Hill, *The religion of Gerrard Winstanley* (1979)

**462** is a brilliantly conceived and executed book. It looks at the emergence of such radical groups as the Diggers, the Ranters and the Muggletonians and sets them against the social and emotional crises engendered by civil war. The first five chapters, examining the privations of the poor and their response, are amongst the most eloquent of all Hill's writings and lead into a series of brilliant vignettes. Hill shows that we must take the ideas of the lunatic fringe seriously, but does not convince that they came near to turning the world upside down. **463** is an edition of the key works of the most readable and moving of the radicals, the Digger leader. This Penguin edition has a lengthy introduction which portrays Winstanley as a very secular figure, an interpretation which has been attacked by others (see articles **X47**, **X131**, **X252**) but which Hill has defended in a *Past and Present* Supplement (**464**).

**465.** B. Capp, *The Fifth Monarchy men* (1972)

**466.** A. L. Morton, *The world of the Ranters* (1970)

**467.** Tai Liu, *Discord in Zion* (1973)

**465** is a very thorough, cautious and readable account and analysis of the origins, distribution, beliefs and practices of the Fifth Monarchists. Perhaps just a little more might have been said about their politics. **466** is a collection of essays on religious radicals in the 1650s and is principally concerned with the Ranters. It gives extensive attention to two rare tracts, Clarkson's *Lost Sheep Found* and Coppe's *Burning Fiery Roll* which have recently been republished in inexpensive facsimile editions by the *Rota* (available from department of Politics, University of Exeter). There is also a good essay on Walwyn. **467** is a very disappointing account of the divisions between presbyterian and independent ministers in the 1640s and of the rise and fall of the Fifth Monarchists in the 1650s.

**468.** W. C. Braithwaite, *The beginnings of Quakerism* (1912, 1955)

**469.** W. C. Braithwaite, *The second period of Quakerism* (1919, 1961)

**470.** H. Barbour, *The Quakers in puritan England* (1964)

**471.** R. Vann, *The social development of English Quakerism* (1969)

**472.** G. Nuttall, *Studies in Christian enthusiasm* (1948)

**468–9** were first published in 1912 and 1919, and the second editions are quite heavily revised. **468** covers the period 1652–60 and **469** 1660–1700. Both volumes are very long, detailed and clear narratives. **468** is straightforwardly chronological, but **469** goes over the period twice: first offering an account of the 'struggle for liberty' and of responses to persecution, and then suggesting an account of internal organisation. In the revised edition, the main body of the text is left unchanged, but there are extensive additional notes, a new introduction to volume 2 replaces introductions in each of the old volumes and there are new and better maps. The main thrust of these changes is to relate Quakerism more fully to the puritan matrix. This is the central thesis explored and vindicated in **470** which covers the years 1625–65. It also offers an excellent account of the social context out of which Quakerism grew, and this in turn is further developed by **471** which attempts a statistical study of the Quakers of Buckinghamshire, Norfolk, and Norwich between 1660 and 1740. **472** is concerned only with the years 1652–6 and with the different senses in which four early leaders – Aldam, Farnworth, Holme and Nayler – experienced the quickening of the Holy Spirit within them.

**473.** G. R. Cragg, *Puritanism in the period of the great persecution* (1957)

**474.** C. R. Whiting, *Studies in English puritanism, 1660–1688* (1931)

**475.** C. G. Bolam and others, *The English presbyterians* (1969)

**476.** F. Bate, *The Declaration of Indulgence, 1672* (1908)

**473** is an excellent survey of the forms of and fluctuations in persecution, and presents a judicious picture of non-conformist responses. It may be that denominational lines are blurred a little too much and that more could have been said about the topography of dissent, but this is an engrossing book. **474** consists of a long series of essays on the organisation, practices and sufferings of early dissenting sects. A work of compassionate antiquarianism still useful for its discussion of the minor sects and of dissenting life and institutions but supplanted on the mainstream by **473**. **475** is a curiously imbalanced book (well over half is on the period 1660–1760 and the pre-1660 period is very skimped), but it contains several penetrating essays. It is at its best in arguing for a distinctive English presbyterianism (and antipathy towards the Scottish frame) and for showing how unitarianism grew out of the divisions within English presbyterianism. **476** is a very thorough, uncomplicated and useful account of the background to the Declaration of Indulgence and the response of the dissenters to it.

## The Roman Catholic Church

**477.** J. Bossy, *The English Catholic community, 1570–1850* (1975)

**478.** J. C. H. Aveling, *The handle and the axe* (1976)

**479.** A. C. F. Beales, *Education under penalty: English Catholic education from the Reformation to the fall of James II* (1963)

**480.** M. Havran, *The Catholics of Caroline England* (1962)

**481.** G. H. Tavard, *The seventeenth-century tradition: a study in recusant thought* (1977)

**477** is a controversial book in the very best sense. It starts from two premisses: that the old catholicism of the pre-Reformation era withered and perished from the reign of Mary, to be replaced by a new catholicism which grew steadily stronger from its inception with the foundation of Douai in 1570 to the restoration of the hierarchy in 1850; and that the best way of viewing the English Catholic community is as one wing of English non-conformity. The book is a brilliant exegesis of this theme, at its very best on the patterns of ritual and on the social institutions that maintained the community's distinct identity. One can challenge the premisses and still learn an immense amount, and be made to think. It is one of the most exciting books of the decade. **478** appeared contemporaneously with it and has been rather eclipsed by it. This is a pity for Aveling has spent many years exploring recusant history and this book pulls together and extends the conclusions from a long series of distinguished articles. If **477** is at root a social history of English catholicism, **478** is its political history, and it covers the period 1534–1828. It too should be read. Between them these two supplant most of the earlier books, but **479–81** retain some independent value. **479** is a study of Roman Catholic schooling between 1547 and 1689. It looks at schools, universities and seminaries abroad, and at the suprising number of clandestine schools at home. The approach marries narrative and analysis very skilfully. **480** is short (and could have been shorter). It discusses catholicism at court and recusancy in the provinces. Caroline attitudes to recusants turn out to resemble modern governments' attitudes to tobacco: it should be discouraged yet retained as a vital source of revenue. **481** looks at the debate amongst recusant theologians over the sufficiency of scripture and over the proper judges of authority within the church. I found it very hard going. Those wishing to extend their knowledge of recusancy should turn to *Recusant History*, a quarterly periodical with a wide range of articles mainly on the first two centuries of recusancy.

## Biographies

**482.** P. Welsby, *George Abbot: the unwanted archbishop* (1962)

**483.** H. R. Trevor-Roper, *Archbishop Laud* (1940)

**484.** V. D. Sutch, *Gilbert Sheldon* (1973)

**485.** E. F. Carpenter, *Thomas Tenison* (1948)

**486.** N. Sykes, *William Wake* (2 vols., 1957)

Two archbishops of Canterbury await reasonable modern biographies: Juxon may yet have time to wait, but R. Beddard has in hand a major work on Sancroft. Meanwhile, only Wake has found his definitive interpreter. **482** deals almost exclusively with Abbot's failure as a courtier and politician: 'a better man than he was an archbishop' is a gentle verdict, but it is allowed to stand by default. There are grounds for thinking him a man of finer intellectual and pastoral mettle. **483** is a brilliant book, the young anti-clerical Trevor-Roper dissecting the most clericist of clerics with wit and poise, but the book is beginning to show its age. **484** is an under-researched and overstated narrative, weak on Sheldon's administrative record, palpably wrong-headed about the Restoration itself (**399**, **426–7**), but with some interesting points on Sheldon's relations with Charles II. It should be read alongside the very severe review article in *Historical Journal* in 1977. **485** is a very full and well-arranged life of a dull man whose archiepiscopate was the longest since Cranmer's. The book falls into three parts: life, government of the church, theology and pastoral ideals. **486** looks at a man who became archbishop after our period, but is included here because Sykes's magnum opus is thematic rather than chronological and thus incorporates a good deal of earlier material. These volumes constitute a virtual general history of the church from 1690 to 1737.

**487.** P. Welsby, *Lancelot Andrewes* (1958)

**488.** M. F. Reidy, *Bishop Lancelot Andrewes* (1955)

**489.** R. B. Knox, *James Ussher* (1967)

**490.** G. Soden, *Godfrey Goodman, bishop of Gloucester* (1953)

**491.** F. H. Huntley, *Bishop Joseph Hall* (1979)

A quiverful of early Stuart episcopal biographies. Andrewes is the man passed over for Canterbury at the death of Bancroft and long revered as a deeply spiritual man. Both the recent books on him tend to downgrade him. **487** sees him as an intellectual courtier and an ecclesiastical fence-sitter, while **488**, based on his sermons, finds his 'learning was broader than it was deep, more extensive than precise' and characterises him as the heir of Luther not Calvin. These accounts fit in well with what we know more generally about the Jacobean period. **489** looks at another theologian whose reputation has remained high. Ussher – archbishop of Armagh in the 1630s – was a royalist who wanted to see episcopacy 'reduced' to its primitive form and who became the hero of the moderate puritans in 1641 and again (after his death) in 1659–60. 'A talented misfit' was how one reviewer described him, and that seems a just verdict. **490** is a disorderly, mannered and often opaque biography of a curious man, who refused to take the oath denouncing popery in the Canons of 1640, was impeached and tried in 1641, but lived in seclusion to die in 1656 declaring that there was no satisfaction outside the faith of the church of Rome. It is worth reading for the account of his trial and of the life of a bishop after the civil war. **491** is a short and not particularly acute explication of the writings of a man who was bishop first of Exeter and then of Norwich whose defence of episcopacy proved an important source of controversy in 1641–2.

**492.** C. J. Stranks, *The life and writings of Jeremy Taylor* (1952)

**493.** E. F. Carpenter, *The protestant bishop* (1956)

**494.** A. T. Hart, *William Lloyd* (1952)

**495.** A. T. Hart, *The life and times of John Sharp, archbishop of York* (1949)

**496.** C. R. Whiting, *Nathaniel Lord Crewe* (1940)

**497.** G. V. Bennett, *White Kennett, bishop of Peterborough* (1957)

**498.** G. V. Bennett, *The tory crisis in church and state* (1975)

**492** is a scholarly and full biography of the divine and Restoration Irish bishop. It gives an excellent and balanced account of Taylor's 'Laudianism' but is shaky on the political background. **493** is a life of Bishop Compton of London, suspended by James II, a key figure in the invasion of William III, and a man usually dismissed as a 'tool' of Danby (following Burnet). Unfortunately, having written a lively life of the dull Tenison (**485**), Carpenter wrote a dull one of the lively Compton. **494–5** are straightforward accounts of two very unremarkable men. **494** is notable for its account of the indecisiveness of decent men in 1688 (Lloyd was one of the 'seven bishops'). **496** is a rather pompous but ultimately quite satisfying account of a man who held the see of Durham for almost fifty years. He is interesting as a collaborator with both James II and William III (he is also famous for his benefaction to Oxford – £200 *p.a.* still spent on strawberries and champagne for the doctors of the University and other dignitaries every year!). **497** takes a fresh look at a polemical Whig bishop and finds him to have been a zealous administrator as well as an inveterate pamphleteer. This book is one of the best accounts of the close relationship of religion and party politics in this period, but is replaced as such by **498**, a brilliant analysis and account of the High Tory bishop Francis Atterbury which is fundamental to any reading list on the politics as on the religion of the period 1688–1730.

**499.** F. Higham, *John Evelyn* (1936)

This brief, rather touching spiritual biography is included as the only worthwhile account of a devout lay anglican in the period.

**500.** F. J. Powicke, *A life of the Reverend Richard Baxter, 1615–1691* (1924)

**501.** F. J. Powicke, *The Reverend Richard Baxter under the cross, 1662–1691* (1927)

**502.** G. Nuttall, *Richard Baxter* (1966).

**503.** W. Lamont, *Richard Baxter and the millenium* (1979)

**504.** I. Morgan, *The non-conformity of Richard Baxter* (1946)

**505.** P. Toon, *God's statesman* (1971)

Despite their confusing titles, **500–1** are volumes 1 and 2 of a single life dividing at 1662. They remain the most thorough account of 'the bishop of Non-Conformity'. **502** is a deceptively slight biography based on years of study and reflection. For most purposes it is to be preferred to **500–1**. But see now **503**, a difficult, demanding but immensely rewarding intellectual biography, not to be attempted by those without a lot of background. **504** is a very lightweight alternative. **505** looks at John Owen, friend and chaplain to Cromwell, vice-chancellor of Oxford University in the 1650s, dissenter in the 1660s. This is a sound, uncomplicated life.

**506.** W. Lamont, *Marginal Prynne* (1963)

**507.** I. Morgan, *Prince Charles' puritan chaplain* (1957)

**508.** R. P. Stearns, *The strenuous puritan* (1954)

Three 'puritan' lives. **506** finds erastian strains as a key to the tergiversations of a quarrelsome, prolix and self-righteous puritan martyr. It reads very well. **507** is a very straightforward and not very probing life of John Preston. **508** is a vigorous and scholarly rehabilitation of the regicide preacher Hugh Peter, excellent on the development of his thought, but perhaps too keen to gloss over the opportunism of his political statements. See also **A2** (p. 179).

**509.** R. L. Greaves, *John Bunyan* (1969)

There are several biographies of Bunyan, but this short, spare, well-documented life and explication of his thought replaces all its predecessors. It needs to be used alongside the suggestive appendix in **462**.

# 7
# ECONOMIC HISTORY

No other section is so well served with textbooks as economic history. There are at least five books which can be happily recommended to senior school students and undergraduates (**510–13, 517**). This is certainly not because all the major problems have been explored, but rather because there are so many sound and thorough monographs and a particularly extensive article literature to build on, because there is reasonable agreement amongst historians on the main features of the period and because there is a clear recognition of the limitations of surviving evidence and of the areas which have not been adequately explored. The great bulk of the work has been descriptive rather than analytical economic history, and work on early modern England has not been much affected/afflicted by econometric studies.

This chapter, like the preceeding one, is arranged topically rather than chronologically, a decision which follows the grain of the scholarship. Economic historians much prefer to write the history of one institution, craft or vegetable over a long period than to relate one to another over a short period. Thus it is easy enough to discover how and by what means coal or glass production expanded, not so easy to find a relationship between them. It is perhaps not surprising that we do not get books on 'The economy of England under James II' but it is surprising that so few local studies have been published which examine the interdependence of different economic activities within particular regions or towns. This is not entirely fair, for there are several important unpublished theses which do so, and some examples have been placed not in this chapter but in chapter 9. But they remain disappointingly few, and are frequently very fragmented, treating agriculture, manufactures and markets quite separately and not placing their interdependence at the heart of the analysis.

There are satisfactory studies of most of the major subjects, although a general work reassessing the nature and decline of 'state control' would be welcome, and a fresh examination of the labour market is overdue. We now know a lot about land use, but the changing pattern of landholding remains obscure, and must be approached through a number of conflicting articles. Both patterns of ownership and forms of tenancy need clarifying. The forthcoming volume 5 of the *Agrarian History of England and Wales, 1640–1740* may resolve this and other problems (perhaps even the problem of pig-farming in the seventeenth century which seems woefully neglected!). I think I know as much as I want about textiles, though it would be nice to know just how many people it employed, but the leather industry, second only to textiles, is a very unknown quantity. Brewing also needs to be studied by someone with a clear head. Otherwise, studies of individual industries are probably less needed than a more thorough study of marketing. Overseas, the only areas in need of major studies are probably the Levant and the Atlantic trade at the end of the period. There is far more to be done on private credit and one could do with more major studies of financiers and merchants to match **618** or **619**. Nonetheless, I suspect that economic historians feel discontent less with the secondary literature of recent years than with the underlying lack of data which will forever condemn them to an inexactitude unbecoming to their profession. Such a discontent would invert the habitual feelings of political and social historians.

## General Works

**510.** L. A. Clarkson, *The pre-industrial economy in England, 1500–1750* (1971)

**511.** B. A. Holderness, *Pre-industrial England: economy and society from 1500–1750* (1976)

**512.** D. C. Coleman, *The economy of England, 1450–1750* (1977)

**513.** C. Wilson, *England's apprenticeship, 1603–1763* (1965)

Four excellent introductory surveys. **510** and **511** are largely interchangeable: both are descriptive rather than analytical, both seek clarity by drawing too static a picture, both cover largely the same ground (agriculture, manufactures, commerce and communications, the role of the government). **511** is clearer on demography and social structure, but **510** is probably a more readable introduction. **512** is shorter, more incisive, more challenging. It achieves a greater sense of change over time by dividing the period at 1650 and treating each major topic separately on both sides of that divide. Its pithiness makes it a superb second book after beginners have got some basic grasp from **510** or **511**. **513** is a different kind of book. It subdivides the shorter span into the three periods – 1603–60, 1660–1700, 1700–63 – and proceeds topically within these divisions. It is far more detailed and fertile in specific insights, but the overall conceptual framework is harder to discern. It is excellent in discussing the multifarious ways in which England followed or imitated the Netherlands, on trade and on social change, but less secure on the effects of inflation and on internal government regulations.

**514.** E. Lipson, *Economic history of England*, vols. 2 and 3 (1931, 1943)

**515.** E. Lipson, *The growth of English society* (1949, 1959)

**516.** C. Hill, *Reformation to industrial revolution* (1967)

**517.** B. Murphy, *A history of the British economy, 1086–1740* (1973)

**518.** P. Gregg, *Black Death to industrial revolution* (1976)

**519.** R. O'Day, *Economy and community* (1975)

Bluntly, these are the textbooks which occupy the substitutes' bench. They are not as good or useful as **510–13**. **514** is a classic and covers the 'Age of mercantilism'. Volume 2 treats industry (textiles, coal and iron only), foreign trade (company by company) and agriculture. Volume 3 examines 'the mercantile system', 'the control of industry' and 'the relief of the poor'. It is static and stodgy but a great mine of information. **515** is a potted version which finds 'the age of mercantilism' – with its 'growth of individualism' and 'the first planned economy' – sandwiched between 'the corporate society' and 'the machine age'. Boldly conceptualised and good for readers who want to exercise their minds on finding the fatal flaws in teleological history. **516** offers the same thesis in a rather different garb. Its attempt to portrary the English Revolution as the decisive turning point in English economic and social history, as the moment when 'the middle ages came to an end', is cleverly and clearly argued, but does not survive close scrutiny. **517** is very nearly in the same league as **510–11** and is a very underrrated textbook. The two chapters spanning 1485–1740 contain over 200 pages and fulfil the author's claim of having written a comprehensive textbook for pre-university students and a basic work of reference for higher-level students. It is at its best in explaining how basic economic concepts help us to understand early modern developments. A second paperback volume covers 1740–1970 and the hardback contains both. **518** is altogether weaker: a series of static accounts of the major topics some of which (e.g. the chapter on price history) is confused and confusing. We trundle along from 'feudalism to modern contractual society', mainly through the mechanism of government action. **519** is a slender and a rather curious work. Calling itself an 'economic and social history of pre-industrial England 1500–1700' it looks in 140 pages at population and price rises, at growth of towns and schools, at the demand for capital and credit, at the plunder of the church and at overseas trade. Some of these chapters are useful summaries of recent literature, but there is no overall theme or logic. There is a documentary appendix which is even more of a ragbag.

**520.** H. C. Darby (ed.), *A new historical geography of England* (1973)

**521.** R. A. Dodgshon and R. A. Butlin (eds.), *An historical geography of England and Wales* (1979)

These two books make a splendid complement to one another. **520** alternates narrative accounts of developments over time 'The age of the improver, 1600–1800' with analyses of the situation at key dates ('England 1600'). Each chapter has five separate divisions (population, the countryside, industry, transport and trade, towns and cities). Regional variations are given full treatment. Each chapter is by one author. **521** has three chapters on the period 1500–1730: agriculture, industry and towns, and population, each by a different author. Both books are recommendable – **521** is more authoritative on towns and demography, but **520** ultimately has better maps, more information, more breadth.

**522.** J. Thirsk and J. P. Cooper (eds.), *Seventeenth-century economic documents* (1970)

**523.** E. Carus-Wilson (ed.), *Essays in economic history*, vol. 1 (1954); vol. 2 (1962)

**522** was produced as a source book for a paper in the final year at Oxford University. It contains, unadorned with commentary or introductions, 800 pages of documents arranged topically. Within each section the texts are laid out chronologically. In their quest for fresh examples and evidence, the editors occasionally by-pass major sources already freely available and this makes for a lack of self-sufficiency (e.g. there is no extract from the poor laws or acts of settlement). It is, however, a most splendid and browsable collection. **523** reprints 'those articles which have proved most in demand among students'. Volume 1 consists entirely of articles from the *Economic History Review*, volume 2 of items from there and elsewhere. Six articles in volume 1 and eight in volume 2 are directly relevant to the seventeenth century

**524.** R. B. Outhwaite, *Inflation in Tudor and Stuart England* (1969)

An admirable brief survey in Macmillan's Studies in Economic and Social History series. It examines the nature and extent of inflation in the period 1500–1650 and comments on its economic consequences. The author is cautious about the sufficiency of either monetarist or 'real' factors, which is refreshing, and his discussion of the chronology and proportions of the problem is very just and nicely judged.

**525.** J. Thirsk, *Economic policy and projects* (1978)

This is a revised version of a series of Ford Lectures at Oxford. It argues that a rising demand for consumer goods was a vital feature of the seventeenth-century economy and stimulated a vast expansion of such rural industries as stocking-knitting, pin-making, starch production, etc. It suggests that there was a highly developed 'market economy' in England long before industrial take-off.

**526.** J. Appleby, *Economic thought and ideology in seventeenth-century England* (1978)

**527.** M. Bowley, *Studies in the history of economic theory before 1870* (1973)

**528.** E. S. Furniss, *The position of the labourer in a system of nationalism* (1920)

**526** is an ambitious and intelligent book which takes as its unargued premiss the rise of the market economy (as discussed in **525**). It then claims to find economic thinkers responding to and rationalising just such a perceived change. There is much of interest, but the author's knowledge of particular contexts of many of the works she discusses is inadequate and weakens the force of her arguments. The first 100 pages of **527** contain essays on the control of the money supply, usury and the 'development of value theory'. The writing is brisk but quite technical. **528** also considers economic theorising. It examines the work of the 'later English mercantilists' of the period 1660–1775. It is arranged topically which limits its usefulness for seventeenth-century specialists, but its discussion of doctrines of employment, of the utility of poverty, of wage theory and of the duties and responsibilities of the state are still the best available.

## Agriculture

**529.** J. Thirsk (ed.), *The agrarian history of England and Wales*, vol. 4; *1500–1640* (1967)

**530.** E. Kerridge, *The agricultural revolution* (1967)

**531.** E. Kerridge, *The farmers of old England* (1973)

**529** is authoritative, challenging and very long. After a survey of regional variations, it contains chapters on (a) farming techniques, (b) enclosing and engrossing, (c) landlords, (d) labourers, (e) marketing, (f) agricultural prices and rents, (g) rural housing. The chapters constituting (d) and (e) by A. M. Everitt are both outstandingly important. Volume 5 of this series, covering the century after 1640 is now in the press and will no doubt be equally definitive. I understand its organisation is more strongly regional. **530** argues that the agricultural revolution took place in the sixteenth and seventeenth centuries and not in the eighteenth and nineteenth. It stresses new forms of land use and new crops rather than technology and changes in the distribution of land. It has been generally felt that the author has a good case but grossly overstates it. **531** is really a shorter version for those who revel in talk of turnips, leguminous grasses and the unpronouncable sainfoin. I have found that as many are attracted as are repelled.

**532.** W. Minchinton (ed.), *Essays in agrarian history*, vol. 1 (1968)

**533.** E. L. Jones (ed.), *Agriculture and economic growth, 1650–1815* (1967)

Two (partially overlapping) collections of essays. **532** includes W. G. Hoskins on harvest fluctuations, M. Havinden on how new techniques could be and were introduced into an open-field area (Oxfordshire), E. Kerridge on turnip husbandry, H. J. Habakkuk on the economic functions of landowners and three articles by R. V. Lennard, E. L. Jones and A. H. John on agricultural change and economic growth after 1660. The articles by Havinden and Jones reappear in **533** which retains seventeenth-century interest through its lengthy introduction.

**534.** J. A. Yelling, *Common fields and enclosure in England, 1450–1750* (1977)

**535.** R. H. Tawney, *The agrarian problem of the sixteenth century* (1912, 1967)

**536.** E. Kerridge, *Agrarian problems in the sixteenth century and after* (1969)

**534**, by a geographer, is an immensely thorough and technical study of the 'spatial and chronological patterns of enclosure', stressing the importance of partial or piecemeal enclosure, and also the effects of enclosure. It examines the latter by comparing patterns of landholding, layout of estates, land use and productivity in both enclosed and surviving common-field areas. This book completely supersedes older books by G. Slater and E. C. K. Gonner. **535** was a very remarkable book in its time, and its attempts to find relationships between law, government, social structure, land distribution and agricultural technology are worthy of imitation. But its central thesis, that by 1600 the English peasantry had lost the battle for survival against economic and social forces antipathetic to their interests, has not stood the test of time. **536** rather exults in finding the flaws in Tawney's argument, and is written without the latter's eloquence or easy comprehension, but it does establish a contrary argument. Both rely to some extent on seventeenth-century evidence and should be consulted. The 1967 reprint of **535** contains a good introductory essay by L. Stone.

**537.** J. Thirsk, *English peasant farming* (1957)

**538.** D. Summers, *The great level* (1976)

**539.** H. C. Darby, *The draining of the Fens* (1940)

**537** looks at Lincolnshire from 1500 to 1914, comparing the changing experiences of smallholders in marsh, clay and upland regions. It is weak in its failure to define a peasant, in its neglect of the records of landowners and on a rather inadequate sampling technique for its extrapolations from inventories. But the hundred pages or so on the seventeenth century are vital to an understanding of the differing experiences of neighbouring groups of farmers. **538–9** concern the draining of the Lincolnshire/Cambridgeshire Fenland. **538** devotes 70 pages, **539** over a hundred to our period. **538** is a straightforward account of the legal, economic and political problems confronting the drainers, while **539** glances at such problems, but stresses the geographical and engineering problems.

**540.** P. A. Pettit, *The royal forests of Northamptonshire, 1558–1714* (1968)

**541.** Lord Leconfield, *Petworth Manor in the seventeenth century* (1954)

**540** looks at another area 'improved' in our period. The first two-thirds examines the activities of the owners and administrators of the woodland, and the conflict of interests between developers and subsistence farmers. The last part studies the economic and demographic pressures on the forest peasants. It is published by the Northamptonshire Record Society. **541** looks at the structure of the manor, at the copyholders, and at the economic activities practised there. It is very much an antiquarian work, preoccupied with picturesque detail (like the number of unringed pigs), but useful as such.

**542.** G. E. Fussell, *The English farm labourer, 1500–1900* (1949)

**543.** G. E. Fussell, *The English dairy farmer, 1500–1900* (1952)

**544.** G. E. Fussell, *Old English farming books from Fitzherbert to Tull, 1523–1730* (1947)

**545.** M. W. Barley, *The English farmhouse and cottage* (1961)

**542–4** are examples of a long series of descriptive works produced by the author over the years. **542** and **543**, based on inventories, lawsuits, etc., describe the homes, furniture, clothing and food of their subject over the ages. **544** is the most important, offering a straightforward account of the changing content and emphasis of the farming manuals. It looks both at books on husbandry and surveying. **545** concentrates on the 'housing revolution' of 1575–1690 (c.f **58** and article **X375**), and treats that period regionally and in three chronological chunks. It is better on farmhouses than on cottages. For most purposes, Barley's chapter on rural housing in **529** supplants it.

## Manufactures

**546.** D. C. Coleman, *Industry in Tudor and Stuart England* (1975)

**547.** S. Jack, *Trade and industry in Tudor and Stuart England* (1977)

**548.** J. U. Nef, *Industry and government in England and France, 1540–1640* (1940, 1957)

**546**, in Macmillan's Studies in Economic and Social History series, is a masterly introduction to the subject. It is built around three main chapters – on urban handicrafts, on the putting-out system mainly in the countryside, and on the 'centralised production' found mainly but not exclusively in mining. It stresses the absence of major technological breakthrough and the importance of endemic underemployment. **547** is longer but less successful and in some ways less comprehensive. It attempts to create an 'overall economic matrix' through which the problem of growth can be explored, and then looks in turn at the contribution of each group of industries. Only ten pages are devoted to marketing. Much time is spent demolishing the ideas of Nef (see **548** and **566**) which is pointless since to my knowledge no textbook in the last twenty years has been inclined to endorse any of the latter's more extravagant claims to have discovered an industrial revolution in our period. **548** is over-schematic but offers a very useful contrast between the crown's direct and indirect involvement with manufacturing in the two countries. It should be read for the incidental details along the route, not for the destination of the argument.

**549.** G. Unwin, *Industrial organisations in the sixteenth and seventeenth centuries* (1904, 1957)

**549** is a thorough history of the rise of the domestic system and of joint stock and chartered companies but is marred by an anachronistic use of 'class' concepts and by a teleological approach. It draws its evidence predominantly from the years before 1600.

**550.** P. Bowden, *The wool trade in Tudor and Stuart England* (1962)

**551.** H. Heaton, *The Yorkshire woollen and worsted industries* (1920, 1965)

**552.** J. de L. Mann, *The cloth industry in the west of England, 1640–1880* (1971)

**553.** A. P. Wadsworth and J. de L. Mann, *The cotton trade and industrial Lancashire, 1600–1730* (1931)

**554.** G. D. Ramsay, *The Wiltshire woollen industry in the 16th and 17th centuries* (1943)

**555.** T. C. Mendenhall, *The Shrewsbury drapers and the Welsh wool trade in the XVI and XVII centuries* (1953)

All the main textile regions have been thoroughly served by capable scholars over the years, except for East Anglia, whose textile history lies mainly in thesis form. **550** is an excellent general work. The first half looks at sheep farming, wool production, modes of production and marketing. The second part is devoted to differing forms of regulation by parliament, staple, licence, etc. and at trade embargoes. **551–5** all devote over a hundred pages to the seventeenth century. Those with time or patience for only one regional study should look at **554**. See also articles **X304**, **X313**, **X314**, **X337**, **X338**.

**556.** J. U. Nef, *The rise of the British coal industry* (2 vols., 1932)

A book which overstates an important case. It shows how coal production rose steeply between 1500 and 1700. It traces coal's emergence as a major industrial and domestic fuel and sees it as a 'fertile field for the new economic order', i.e. capitalism. The chapters on expansion of production, on the marketing of coal, on the substitution of coal for wood and the ownership of the mines are still vital. But others, like 'an early industrial revolution', have been much criticised.

**557.** W. H. B. Court, *The rise of the Midlands industries, 1600–1838* (1938)

**558.** M. B. Rowlands, *Masters and men* (1975)

**559.** D. Hey, *The rural metalworkers of the Sheffield region* (1972)

**560.** H. Hamilton, *The English brass and copper industries* (1926)

The metal-working industries are less fully served than textiles, but what has been written tends to be livelier and more readable. **557** has weathered exceptionally well and remains a splendid study of the distinctive geographical and social characteristics of the West Midlands which allowed the precocious development of iron, coal and glass industries in the area. **558** uses wills and inventories to offer a clearer outline of the organisation of the industry in the same region but it supplements rather than supplants. **559** uses the same sources to show how the cutlers, scythe-makers and nail-makers of the Sheffield region all engaged in agriculture to a marked degree in addition to their crafts. **560** takes us back to the Midlands, and the four chapters devoted to our period explain the breakdown of the monopoly and discuss the organisations of the industry, particularly in Birmingham itself.

**561.** D. C. Coleman, *The English paper industry, 1495–1860* (1958)

**562.** E. S. Godfrey, *The development of English glassmaking, 1560–1640* (1975)

**563.** G. H. Kenyon, *The glass industry in the Weald* (1967)

**564.** R. Davis, *The rise of the English shipping industry* (1962)

**561** devotes nearly a hundred pages to the seventeenth century, examining organisation, markets and government regulations. It is very well done. **562–3** are sharply contrasted. **562** devotes half of its space to an account of the glass industry from the arrival of Huguenot refugees in the 1560s through various patents to the eve of the civil war; in the second part it looks at the structure of the industry, at technological problems, questions of capital and credit and at the range of manufactured goods. It has been criticised for not being sufficiently integrated and for allowing the detail to get out of control. It is, however, lively in comparison with **563**, the work of an archaeologist and historian of technology which looks at the manufacturing processes and range of products, and which identifies the sites of Kent and Sussex glasshouses. It covers the thirteenth to the seventeenth centuries. It is a relief to browse afresh in a masterly study of the evolution of English shipping (**564**). It is clear and authoritative on the ownership, management and manning of ships, on the rate of increase in English tonnage, and also on the comparative importance of coastal, European and transoceanic shipping. The sections on ship design and on the craft of shipbuilding are a little less satisfactory, but this is still a marvellous book.

## Commerce

**565.** J. Chartres, *Internal trade in England, 1500–1750* (1977)

**566.** T. S. Willan, *The inland trade* (1976)

**567.** J. Crofts, *Packhorse, waggon and post* (1967)

**565** is a most useful essay in the Studies in Economic and Social History series. It looks at the organisation and content of domestic trades, at transport and the 'technology' of communications. It lacks an adequate conclusion estimating the contributions of improvements in internal communications, credit, etc. to economic growth in this period. It is also rather congested at times. **566** is a collection of essays of which one on the movement of goods in Elizabethan England (by road, sea and river) is also useful for our period, and one on provincial shops in the seventeenth century is fundamental. **567** is a rather anecdotal, descriptive book that is best for the incidental details about the variegated activities of common carriers. It covers the Tudor and Stuart periods.

**568.** W. Albert, *The turnpike road system, 1667–1840* (1972)

**569.** T. S. Willan, *River navigation in England, 1600–1750* (1930)

**570.** T. S. Willan, *English coasting trade, 1600–1750* (1938)

**571.** J. R. Ward, *The finances of canal building in the eighteenth century* (1974)

No-one has explored the roads of early modern England, though the early chapters of **568** provide basic information (see also article **X305**). It is a good subject for someone. **569–70** both tell a story of expansion. **569** looks at river improvements by patent, commission, and Act of Parliament as well as at engineering problems and the nature of river traffic. **571** is essentially an eighteenth-century work but contains important revisions of **569**.

**572.** R. Davis, *English overseas trade, 1500–1700* (1973)

**573.** G. D. Ramsay, *English overseas trade during the centuries of emergence* (1957)

**574.** W. Minchinton (ed.), *The growth of English overseas trade* (1969)

**572** is a brilliantly concise statement of the switch from northern Europe to the Mediterranean and the colonies, and from dependence on others to the triumphalism of the Navigation Acts. It is in Macmillan's Studies in Economic and Social History series. **573**, which treats 1450–1750, is less analytical, and is more discursive (more a collection of essays than an integrated study), but it is a masterly summary of much English and continental scholarship. There is a particularly good chapter on smuggling. **574** is a collection of reprinted articles covering the seventeenth and eighteenth centuries.

**575.** B. Supple, *Commercial crisis and change, 1600–1642* (1959)

**576.** C. Wilson, *Profit and power* (1957)

**575** is an excellent though quite 'difficult' study of London trade fluctuations, the influences on them at home and abroad (particularly monetary problems) and the response in government policy. **576** is a study of 'the interdependence of sea-power and trade'. It examines Anglo-Dutch relations in the period 1651–67 (oddly it largely ignores the third war) together with a lengthy introduction on English commercial interests and thought in the early seventeenth century. It supplants an earlier book by G. Edmundson.

**577.** W. R. Scott, *The constitution and finance of joint stock companies* (3 vols., 1912)

**578.** L. A. Harper, *The English navigation laws* (1939)

**579.** C. M. Andrews, *British committees, commissions and councils of trade* (1908)

Three elderly, portly, but remarkably spry works. **577** is a masterpiece too little used nowadays. Volume 1 offers a chronological survey of the rise and (often fall) of joint stock enterprises between 1553 and 1730, placing them in a wide economic context. It contains important considerations of the crisis of 1620–5, of the Stop of the Exchequer, and other events. Volumes 2 and 3 treat the companies in turn: foreign trade, colonisation, fishing, extractive industries, drainage schemes (vol. 2); water supply, street lighting, postal services, manufactures, banking, insurance and a miscellany in Ireland and Scotland (vol. 3). The context is again very broad: a fundamental work, very easy to read and use. **578** is principally concerned with the period 1660–96 and falls into four parts: the origin of the laws, enforcement in England and in the colonies, consequences. It is most useful nowadays on matters of enforcement. **579** is mercifully short, but very earnest. It examines conciliar and parliamentary supervision of trade and life in the colonies.

**580.** J. S. Kepler, *The exchange of Christendom* (1976)

**581.** R. Davis, *The trade and shipping of Hull, 1500–1700* (1964)

**580** is an important study of the way England benefited from its neutrality in the Thirty Years' War and from the need of the continental powers to find commercial intermediaries. The role of Dover as a burgeoning entrepôt is examined, together with the effects on English shipping and on the Mint. The period covered is 1612–51 and the chapters on the 1640s are particularly illuminating. **581** is a study of what the author calls 'the one provincial port that retained some importance throughout the period'. It is almost the only monograph on a port as a port. Those interested in other outports should look at **720**, **721** and **723**.

**582.** K. R. Andrews, *Elizabethan privateering* (1964)

**583.** A. Friis, *Alderman Cockayne's project* (1927)

**582** is important for the seventeenth century because it shows what huge profits were made by the London merchant community from the privateering war with Spain, money then being available for investment in America and the East. **583** is ostensibly a study of a failed attempt in the 1610s to change the nature of the English cloth industry, but it is in fact still the fullest and best general account of the organisation of cloth exports in the half-century before 1640.

**584.** R. W. K. Hinton, *The eastland trade and the common weal* (1959)

**585.** S. E. Aström, *From cloth to iron* (1965)

**586.** J. F. Fedorowicz. *England's Baltic trade in the early seventeenth century* (1979)

**587.** J. M. Price, *The tobacco adventure to Russia* (1961)

**584** is concerned principally with the period 1620–80 and with the administrative and political aspects of the company's history. Thus it contains an excellent treatment of the Navigation Acts and of the implications of the expansion of direct royal authority in international relations for the autonomy of the company. It is weakest on the organisation and nature of the commerce itself, for which see **585**, a study of Anglo-Baltic trade in the late seventeenth century (1670–98), notable for its wealth of important statistical tables (which relies overwhelmingly on the Sound Tolls). **586** is a narrow study of the changing patterns of Anglo-Polish trade as the Poles failed to meet English demand for naval supplies and could no longer afford to import broadcloth. **587** is a wider study than its title suggests, examining the whole of Anglo-Russian trade in the late seventeenth century and the composition and interests of the London merchants involved.

**588.** A. C. Wood, *A history of the Levant Company* (1935)

You can tell that this is a work by the devoted Nottingham antiquarian who produced **715**. It is always sensible and clear, but is clogged by detail and it chronicles rather than analyses the changes. It is, indeed, in many ways, of more use to the diplomatic than to the economic historian. Only one-third of the book concerns the seventeenth century.

**589.** K. N. Chaudhuri, *The English East India Company* (1965)

**590.** K. N. Chaudhuri, *The trading world of Asia and the English East India Company, 1660–1760* (1978)

**591.** W. Foster, *England's quest for eastern trade* (1933)

**592.** Bal Krishna, *Commercial relations between India and England, 1601–1757* (1924)

**593.** P. J. Thomas, *Mercantilism and the East India Company* (1926)

**589** covers the period 1600–40 and examines both the activities of the company and its business methods. There is little, however, on the company's troubled relations with the crown. **590** is a massive and broader book. It is analytical and topical rather than chronological and therefore difficult to use for our period alone. The title is a clear guide to the contents, and econometric methods are deployed. **591** is a straightforward account of the explorations of the east and their rationale. **592**, a discussion of the functioning of trade, is largely superseded by **590**. **593** is better on the problems of bullion exports and the import of Indian textiles than the debate these problems inspired.

**594.** K. G. Davies, *The Royal Africa Company* (1957)

**595.** A. J. Barker, *The African link: British attitudes to the Negro in the era of the Atlantic slave trade* (1978)

**596.** R. Pares, *Merchants and planters* (1960)

**597.** E. E. Rich, *Hudson's Bay Company*, vol. 1: *1670–1713* (1961)

**594** covers the period 1672–1713 and is an exhaustive treatment of every aspect of the organisation of the company (and of the slave traders) at home and abroad. **595** draws its evidence mainly from the eighteenth century but it replaces earlier work on the subject. It is at its best on the attitudes of merchants and travellers rather than those of the public at home. **596** looks at the character of English connections with the West Indies (again mainly for the eighteenth century), while **597** is a multi-volume account of English interests in the north-west of America. The first 400 pages cover the period from the charter to 1713.

**598.** A. P. Newton, *The colonising activities of the early puritans* (1914)

**599.** L. B. Wright, *Religion and empire* (1943)

**600.** T. K. Rabb, *Enterprise and empire* (1967)

**601.** H. C. Porter, *The inconstant savage* (1979)

**602.** D. B. Quinn, *England and the discovery of America, 1481–1620* (1974)

**603.** W. F. Craven, *The dissolution of the Virginia Company* (1932)

**604.** W. F. Craven, *The Virginia Company of London, 1606–1624* (1957)

**605.** K. Andrews, N. Canny and P. Hair (eds.), *The westward enterprise* (1978)

There is a vast literature on the English in North America. Here we can only be concerned with those activities and attitudes which took men there or kept them in touch with the metropolitan country. **598** is still much used but should be pensioned off and replaced by something more up-to-date. Subtitled *The last phase of the Elizabethan struggle*, it offers a vast chronological account of the puritan ventures in the West Indies (particularly Providence Island) and New England. It assumes far too much similarity and militancy of aim and achievement. **599**, based largely on propaganda tracts produced to create a sentiment sympathetic to overseas settlement, is a naive and simplistic work. **600** hides its naivety in a more brazen garb. The author fed into a computer the names of 6,000 investors in overseas ventures between 1575 and 1630, and then tried to establish patterns. It concludes that the most profitable ventures were those dominated by merchant investors, the most unsuccessful those dominated by non-merchants. But its categorisation is highly unsophisticated and dubious, and there is a total absence of any sense of change over time. **601** is a diffuse, awkward but often shrewd and sensitive study of changing English attitudes to the American Indian between 1500 and 1650. **602** is the author's collected articles and is overwhelmingly concerned with the sixteenth century and stops where successful colonisation begins, but is vital on the background. **603** is a detailed study of the failure of the Virginia Company on both sides of the Atlantic. It is concerned with the years 1618–23. **604** is a hard-to-obtain pamphlet, part of a series produced to mark the 350th anniversary of the foundation of Jamestown. It is a straightforward introduction in some 50 pages. **605** is a *Festschrift* to D. B. Quinn and is subtitled *English activities in Ireland, the Atlantic and America, 1480–1650.* Most of the fourteen essays deal with the latter. The range is considerable, from H. Kearney's very general piece arguing that historians have paid too much attention to New England and not enough to Virginia and the West Indies, via ones on 'social control' in Ireland and Virginia, 1550–1650, or on the transfer of English law to Virginia, 1606–50, to essays on key moments as in Virginia, 1609–10, or in Massachusetts, 1630–1.

**606.** G. L. Beer, *The origins of the British colonial system, 1578–1660* (1908)

**607.** G. L. Beer, *The old colonial system, 1660–1754* (vols. 1 and 2, 1933)

The colonial system is defined as 'that complex system of regulations by means of which, though to a different extent, the economic structures of both metropolis and colony were moulded to conform to the prevailing ideal of a self-sufficient Empire'. **606** looks at its origins, and is still useful for its discussion of the regulations of tobacco, and at the colonial responses to parliament's victory in the civil war. **607** is a very thorough study of the effects of the Navigation Acts and looks in turn at the various parts of the West Indies and at each of the early mainland colonies.

## Public and Private Finance

**608.** F. C. Dietz, *English public finance, 1558–1642* (1932)

**609.** R. Ashton, *The crown and the money market, 1603–1640* (1960)

**608** is the second part of a longer work commencing in 1485. It combines a chronological account of the history of revenue and expenditure and of attempts at reform with a series of 'special studies in revenue and expenditure' – customs farming, impositions, etc. It is lucid, underestimates the problems of handling some of its sources, and is not always reliable. **609** is an even more lucid and far more masterful survey of the operation of government credit which offers a gloomy diagnosis and prognosis of early Stuart finances. More agreeable to read than one is entitled to expect any book on finance to be.

**610.** M. Ashley, *Financial and commercial policies under the Cromwellian protectorate* (1934)

The author's first and best book. It is still the only work on public finance and public credit in the 1650s, and remains useful on the government's attempts to regulate trade and shipping. The treatment of the Navigation Acts is sensible but has been superseded.

**611.** C. D. Chandaman, *English public revenues, 1660–1688* (1975)

**612.** P. M. G. Dickson, *The financial revolution, 1689–1756* (1967)

**611** is authoritative. It treats each source of revenue in turn and then assembles the information to describe the course of royal finances over the period. It concludes that there was little wrong with the Restoration financial settlement that a little more prudence could not have coped with. It is also an excellent study of fiscal administration (cf. **97–99**, **101**). **612** is a brilliant analysis of the origins and management of the national debt and of the 'social structure' of the ownership of the debt. Its argument is of wide significance for political, constitutional and social historians.

**613.** Sir J. Clapham, *The Bank of England* (vol. I, 1944)

**614.** R. D. Richards, *The early history of banking in England* (1929)

**615.** A Feavearyear, *The pound sterling* (1932, 1963)

**616.** J. R. Horsefield, *British monetary experiments, 1650–1720* (1962)

**617.** Ming-Hsun Li, *The great recoinage of 1696–9* (1963)

**613** takes the story from 1694 to 1797 with a long prelude on the antecedents of the Bank (though **614** is still the only full account of these). It is clear, authoritative, and subsumes its predecessors. **615** has four chapters on the seventeenth century, a period which saw the first paper currency to be floated and 'the first credit inflation'. **616** looks in turn at the financial background (including price history) and then first at the story of gold, silver and paper currencies. There is a particularly good section on land banks. All four are written by historians with the kind of mind and probity one would expect in a bank manager. **617**, alas, is very wayward, disorganised and narrowly focused.

**618.** D. C. Coleman, *Sir John Bankes, 1627–1699* (1963)

**619.** C. Clay, *Public finance and private wealth* (1978)

**620.** W. Letwin, *Sir Josiah Child, merchant economist* (1959)

**618** looks at a man who 'governed the affairs of the greatest mercantile corporation in the country, the East India Company, and of its lesser cousin, the Royal Africa Company' and who was variously engaged in trade and finance (public and private) from the Protectorate to the reign of William III, and amassed a substantial fortune in land and property'. Such a man, an MP and JP, fortunate in his friends (Pepys and Locke), is also fortunate to have found so able a biographer. **619** is also a rounded study of a financier – Sir Stephen Fox (1627–1716) – and is a considerable addition to our knowledge of royal financial institutions. **620** is a short study of the economic thought of the greatest of all merchant-financiers. It is agreeably severe and dispassionate in its dissection of his economic thought.

**621.** W. Gough, *The rise of the entrepreneur* (1969)

This book was a miscalculation by a man who wrote pleasantly and shrewdly on political thought. Its attempt to find the capitalist at work in the period 1540–1640 in the textile, metallurgical, coal, alum, glass industries, etc. was premature and weakly conceptualised, but it does contain a great deal in useful detail on less well-known enterprises. See also **A5** (p. 179).

# 8
# SOCIAL HISTORY

If economic historians have done very well to achieve respectability through tilling some very intractable soil, it must be said that social historians have squandered what few resources they possess. In David Nicholl's nineteenth-century volume in this series, the chapter on social history was the longest and his comments reveal it to be the liveliest and most active field. By contrast, there is little distinguished work in seventeenth-century social history, although there are some very honourable exceptions (e.g. **637–9**, **650**, **682**). There is one quite satisfactory area – population history. A few years ago it was fashionable to say that historical demographers were more interested in methodology than in the product of their analyses, but this would now be largely untrue. The work inspired by the Cambridge Group for the History of Population and Social Structure has generated an impressive body of work, and the results of their most ambitious projects are due to be published in the next few years. Those interested in this aspect should not, however, rely wholly on the books and collected articles cited below but try to find a complete run of *Population Studies* and *Local Population Studies*, where many important articles are to be found.

Our knowledge of English social structure, by comparison, is very blurred. The use of titles, the designation of status, the mingling of honorific and functional modes of address by contemporaries all make for difficulties. The additional importation of notion of class seems highly dubious and has certainly in practice made matters worse. In general, historians have tried to define social status by applying to individuals in the past various criteria testable from surviving evidence. This is to violate the criteria used by contemporaries who were able to apply tests not available to us. The first thing we need to do is to be more sensitive to contemporary vocabulary and conceptualisation. It may be inconvenient for us that they coined a term to conjoin knights, esquires and gentlemen (gentry) but not to conjoin 'mere' gentlemen and yeomen, or yeomen and urban master-craftsmen (who seem to us to share more in common), but it is of first importance that they did not do so. That new social perceptions led to the rise of new terms of social reference can be seen by the emergence of the term 'aristocracy' as a social (as against political) designation in the seventeenth and early eighteenth centuries, and the establishment of the term 'squire' for those who wished to retain the notion of gentility as a quality rooted in the ownership of land, after the latter had been debased by its assumption by urban and professional *arrivistes*.

Without a proper understanding of the conceptions of status and of the organisation of society in this period, we can hardly expect to understand the nature of social tensions and conflict or of the forms of social control and their triumph. This aspect of social history falls very particularly and lamentably short of what has been achieved for nineteenth-century England or seventeenth-century France. One theme of the social history which has been more competently treated is the history of social institutions. We know quite a lot about how the poor laws were and were not implemented, for example, though much of the writing is dull and one looks yearningly at Olwen Hufton's *The poor in eighteenth-century France* for an example of what can be done. Historians of crime are in a rather more precarious state. There are dire enough warnings in print about the hazards of uncritically using legal records as social documents, of assuming that the incidence of prosecutions is related to the incidence of crime, or of assuming that one can write a history of 'crime' rather than a history of felonies, misdemeanours or trespasses, but all such warnings are still regularly ignored. I can only say of the history of education, that the great bulk of it seems to be quite extraordinarily tedious. It if were not for the brilliant work of Keith Thomas – in his book on popular religion and magical beliefs, in innumerable articles on attitudes to old age, sexuality, laughter, etc., and in his major forthcoming work on man's attitude to the natural world – there would appear to be little immediate prospect of any amelioration of this overall position. But his work both demonstrates what can be achieved, and suggests subtle and creative ways into and beyond the intractable and often sparse sources.

## General Works

**622.** P. Laslett, *The world we have lost* (1965, 1971)

A very remarkable and precocious work, springing from the early investigations of the Cambridge Group for the History of Population and Social Structure. It examines the family and the household – size, age, distribution, sexual conduct, vulnerability to famine and pestilence – the physical and mental horizons of the village community, social stratification and the distribution of power and authority within the community. It often runs ahead of the evidence and across the conclusions of more recent work, and there are many factual slips (though far less than in the first edition of 1965 which should be avoided). But it is an immensely stimulating and eye-opening book which most lively senior school students and undergraduates seem to enjoy.

**623.** C. Bridenbaugh, *Vexed and troubled Englishmen, 1590–1642* (1968)

**624.** W. Notestein, *The English people on the eve of colonisation* (1954)

**625.** E. Trotter, *Seventeenth-century life in a country parish* (1919)

**623–4** are both books written to explain to American students why conditions were so intolerable in early-seventeenth-century England that thousands wished to escape to a new life in the New World. Both are descriptive social histories based on printed and literary sources, and both are rather lachrymose, but I have always found **623** more useful and evocative than have the purists. The recent paperback reprint of **624** should not make anyone think it is a book with much to teach us nowadays, though it is urbane and clear. **625** derives mainly from North Riding parish and quarter sessions records and is stronger on village government than village life (it really supplements **81**). It is, however, a straightforward, effective narrative and those who want to find out how constables, surveyors of the highway or hogringers were chosen or what they did, should treat this as their starting point.

**626.** A. Macfarlane, *Reconstructing historical communities* (1977)

**627.** A. Macfarlane, *Origins of English individualism* (1978)

**626–7** are by a man who began life as a historian and has become a leading social anthropologist. His field-work in Nepal together with his deep understanding of anthropological techniques have led him to re-evaluate the social history of early modern England. In **626** he demonstrates new techniques for collecting, breaking down and then reintegrating historical records in a way which makes it possible to ask the kind of questions anthropologists and sociologists would ask of present-day societies. It is both a handbook for local historians and a book full of suggestions about the nature of early modern rural communities. If **626** shows the virtues of detailed studies of individual villages, **627** is a bold (some may say brash) attempt to reinterpret the experience of the people of rural England from the twelfth to the eighteenth centuries. It argues that England never had a 'peasantry' in anthropologists' sense of the word, and that the early modern period witnessed no fundamental shift of experience or values in the English countryside. It is a brilliant polemic, even if at times it appears to be tilting at windmills.

### Demography and Family Structure

**628.** E. A. Wrigley, *Population and history* (1969)

**629.** T. H. Hollingsworth, *Historical demography* (1969, 1976)

**630.** J. D. Chambers, *Population, economy and society in pre-industrial England* (1972)

These are the three basic introductions to demographic history. **628** introduces the subject of historical demography, discusses the techniques, and suggests some of the main conclusions which are emerging. It is important both in explaining and justifying the subject, and in that the largest single group of examples are drawn from early modern England. **629** is a volume in the Sources of History series and it examines both the problem of each kind of evidence and the various techniques devised for handling the evidence. Once again, early modern England is a favoured source for illustrating its themes. **630** is the briskest and clearest synthesis of the conclusions deriving from the work which has been done. Its emphasis on the comparative importance in changes in the death rate rather than in the birth rate is likely to be challenged by the forthcoming study by the Cambridge Group who have collated information from over 400 parishes for the period 1538–1841 (previewed in the chapter by R. Smith in **521**).

**631.** E. A. Wrigley (ed.), *An introduction to English historical demography* (1965)

**632.** D. C. Glass and D. C. Eversley (eds.), *Population in history* (1965)

**633.** D. C. Glass and R. Revelle (eds.), *Population and social change* (1972)

**634.** P. Laslett, *Family life and illicit love in earlier times* (1977)

**635.** M. Drake, *Population in industrialisation* (1969)

**636.** P. Slack *et al.*, *The plague reconsidered* (1977)

These are six volumes of essays which collectively constitute the core of the case-study material upon which our knowledge of demographic history of the period is based. **631** is a discussion of the techniques developed for studying population history before and during the English industrial revolution. There are chapters on aggregative analysis and family reconstitution and on ways of establishing social structure of a small community from lists of inhabitants. D. C. Eversley writes on 'population history and local history'. **632** and **634** contain a number of reprinted and revised articles covering several centuries and continents. **633** constitutes the papers from two international conferences. **635** is a collection of reprinted articles with an excellent introduction. See above all Wrigley on Colyton in **632**, **633** and **635**, Glass on London in **633**, and Laslett on Clayworth and Cogenhoe in **634**. **636** is a supplement produced by *Local Population Studies.* It contains three studies of the origins and effects of the plague in Bristol, Eyam and Colyton and three essays on medical aspects of the plague. All deal with the sixteenth and seventeenth centuries. For key articles on historical demography, see also **X343**, **X345**, **X381**, **X401–3**.

**637.** A. B. Appleby, *Famine in Tudor and Stuart England* (1978)

**638.** D. Levine, *Family formation in an age of nascent capitalism* (1977)

**639.** V. Skipp, *Crisis and development* (1977)

A second generation of demographic studies is now emerging which relates demographic change to broader economic and social developments. **637** argues conclusively for extensive deaths from famine in Cumberland and Westmorland in the 1590s and the 1620s, and sets this against a very wide discussion of the geography and economy of the region. Appleby's suggestions that dearth caused high mortality elsewhere (notably in London), and his account of the disappearance of dearth are also invaluable. **638** is more ambitious. Through a series of detailed studies of parishes in Leicestershire, Devon and Essex between 1600 and 1850, it attempts to correlate demographic experience with the particular pattern of employment prevailing in any given area. It is a much more subtle thesis than its rather aggressive title might imply. **639** is the most imaginative book of all, the product of a large number of microscopic investigations by evening classes throughout the Midlands. It is subtitled 'an ecological case study of the Forest of Arden, 1570–1674', and shows how a growing population experienced a sharp Malthusian attack in the 1610s, and that recovery and further expansion could only take place after a major restructuring of the agrarian economy. It is a book which is short, difficult, but deeply rewarding.

**640.** L. A. Clarkson, *Death, disease and famine in pre-industrial England* (1975)

This is a well-intentioned book which fails to make its mark. Based entirely on secondary and printed materials, it examines the high and fluctuating mortality of early modern England and looks at the causes of that pattern (particularly at epidemics and at the effects of dearth). It also looks at human responses to the sudden and terrifying peaks of mortality. Since it does not use the right kinds of evidence, the result is unconvincing and superficial. It might still capture the imagination of students frightened off by the sight of tables in **637**.

**641.** L. Stone, *The family, sex and marriage in England, 1500–1800* (1976, 1979)

**642.** L. Schucking, *The puritan family* (1929, translated into English, 1969)

**641** is Stone's brashest, most wayward and most challenging and thought-provoking book to date. In over 800 pages hardback (there is now a slimline paperback) he argues for a fundamental shift in the nature of the family in England between the terminal dates. It is a study of 'the biological, sociological, political, economic, psychological and sexual' aspects of family life and of their change over time, and it deals with all social groups. It contains some of the worst distortions of evidence, some of the least credible assumptions and some of the most banal statements ever committed to paper by a professor of history. It must be read alongside the devastating review by Alan Macfarlane (article **X374**). But, after all allowance has been made, it is an immensely suggestive and imaginative work, built around a thesis which contains an irreducible core of truth. **642** is very modest by comparison, based almost entirely on diaries and sermons, but with a definition of puritanism so wide as to include most middling-sort and gentry-sort of Englishmen. It looks at domestic and sex roles within marriage, at parental attitudes, and at the relationships of masters and servants. The best part is the concluding section which looks for evidence of these attitudes in action in the writings of Milton, Bunyon, Defoe and Richardson.

**643.** R. Thompson, *Women in seventeenth-century America and England* (1974)

**644.** I. Pinchbeck and M. Hewitt, *Children in English society*, vol. I: *from Tudor times to the 18th century* (1969)

**645.** A. Macfarlane, *The family life of Ralph Josselin* (1970)

**643** is an interesting but premature book, based too exclusively on printed sources. It contrasts the way the imbalanced sex-ratios, radically new economic opportunities and a decisive puritan ethic transformed the position of women within the family and the community in New England and Virginia as against what happened in metropolitan England. **644** is a disappointing work in another sense. It is a rather dull assemblage of facts about the decline of a caring community. Those interested in this subject will learn far more from the over-schematised but highly sensitive study by P. Ariès, *Centuries of childhood*, which, however, is mainly concerned with France. **645**, 'an essay in historical anthropology', looks at the social life of a seventeenth-century yeoman–parson and is outstandingly good on attitudes to birth, adolescence, marriage and death within that milieu. There is also a most useful brief essay on diary-keeping in seventeenth-century English. The vast diary itself has since been published by the British Academy, in an edition prepared by Macfarlane.

**646.** J. Goody, J. Thirsk and E. P. Thompson (eds.), *Family and inheritance* (1976)

This is a pioneering series of expanded conference papers covering different aspects of inheritance and the transmission of property in western Europe, 1200–1800. Those essays with seventeenth-century English connections include C. Howell and M. Spufford on peasant inheritance customs in the Midlands and in Cambridgeshire respectively, and a 140-page blockbuster by J. P. Cooper on patterns of inheritance and settlement by great landowners in England, France, Spain and elsewhere between the fifteenth and eighteenth centuries.

**647.** G. R. Quaife, *Wanton wenches and wayward wives* (1979)

Despite the silly title, this is 'a highly detailed study of illicit sex amongst the peasantry of Somerset between 1601 and 1660'. It is pleasantly written, quotes extensively from the depositions contained in ecclesiastical and county court records, does not overstate or attempt any spurious quantification. Its source-criticism could have been much more rigorous, but its conclusions are mostly convincing and constitute a considerable repudiation of the contentions of **641** about the moral attitudes of magistrates and commonalty.

## Social Structure

**648.** Sir A. Wagner, *English genealogy* (1960, 1972)

**649.** D. Mathew, *The social structure of Caroline England* (1947)

**650.** A. M. Everitt, *Change in the provinces* (1969)

Do not be deterred by the title of **648**, which is broadly conceived and readable. Part IV, the bulkiest, analyses 'the social framework' and is particularly useful for the changing conceptions of status during our period. Other important sections deal with the assimilation of foreigners, sources for the study of genealogy, and the historiography of the subject. **649** began life as some exceptionally quirky Ford Lectures in Oxford. Many fascinating details emerge, but the overall conceptualisation is rather wayward. **650** is an excellent pamphlet which looks at 'the anatomy of provincial life' (diversity, insularity, continuity) and at conservative and dynamic elements within the social structure (including the author's fullest discussion to date of the urban and professional 'pseudo-gentry'). This is an indispensable work.

**651.** L. Stone, *The crisis of the aristocracy, 1558–1641* (1965, 1967)

**652.** L. Stone, *Family and fortune* (1973)

These works are connected. **651** is a blockbuster, no less than an attempt both to anatomise the political elite of English during a century of rapid change, and to explain the long-term causes of the civil war in terms of the relative decline in the military power, financial resources, territorial possessions, self-confidence, prestige and authority of the aristocracy. It is brilliantly conceptualised and sustained, but based on some spectacularly weak use of evidence and some very dubious assumptions (which begin with the title: why the 'aristocracy', a term with no social resonance in his period? – Why not 'the crisis of the peerage?') The subsequent 350-page paperback is a brilliant reduction of the 750-page original and will serve most people's needs (but see articles **X80** and **X346**). **652** is a complement to **651**, offering one major study (the Cecil earls of Salisbury) and four minor ones illustrating the themes of its predecessor with regard to aristocratic finance.

**653.** L. Stone, *Social change and revolution in England, 1540–1640* (1965)

**654.** M. E. Finch, *Five Northamptonshire families* (1956)

**655.** A. Simpson, *The wealth of the gentry, 1540–1660* (1961)

**656.** G. E. Mingay, *The gentry* (1976)

**653** is a source-book and gives edited highlights from the ferocious rumpus amongst historians in the 1950s known as 'the gentry controversy' which originated in Tawney's famous article relating the rise of the gentry to the causes of the civil war. Most historians would now see the debate as being argued from false premisses and on inadequate evidence by all parties, and the book's interest is now mainly historiographical, and for those who enjoy blood sports! 'An erring colleague is not an Amalekite to be smitten hip and thigh', wrote Tawney at one point, and with good reason. **654–5** are irenical works inspired by the debate and by the clamour for case-studies. **654** (published by the Northants Record Society) examines the economic fortunes of five families, concentrating on estate management and family settlements. It assumes rather too much technical background in its readers but is otherwise excellent. **655** looks at a rising lawyer, a rising merchant, a courtier in and out of favour, and a cluster of 'mere' landowners, all in East Anglia. Both books conclude that prosperity was the reward of prudence, not of a progressive mentality. **656** attempts a general history of the gentry and succeeds in doing little more than summarising the extant secondary literature without imposing a coherent overall theme. It is much better on gentry finances than on conceptions of status, lifestyle or duties to the commonwealth.

**657.** M. E. James, *English politics and the concept of honour, 1485–1642* (1978)

**658.** J. W. Stoye, *English travellers abroad, 1604–1667* (1952)

**657** is running out of steam by the early seventeenth century, but it is a deeply informed and thoughtful account of the transformation of the gentry's self-image from a chivalric to a civic basis. It is a *Past and Present* supplement. **658** is a sensitive study of one aspect of the gentry lifestyle – the grand tour. It explains its purpose and ponders the influence of foreign travel on English politics and culture.

**659.** M. Campbell, *The English yeoman under Elizabeth and the early stuarts* (1942)

An analysis of the place of the yeoman in English society and economy – their status, wealth, work, lifestyle, values and role in local government. It is still a basic and absorbing work.

## Urban Studies

**660.** P. Clark and P. Slack, *English towns in transition, 1500–1700* (1976)

**661.** J. Patten, *English towns, 1500–1700* (1978)

**662.** P. Clark (ed.), *The early modern town: a reader* (1976)

**663.** P. Clark and P. Slack (eds.), *Crisis and order in English towns, 1500–1700* (1972)

Our knowledge of urban history has been transformed in recent years, though the number of detailed case studies in print remains far too small. **660** is an excellent introductory survey, lucid, wide-ranging and shrewd (it is in Oxford University Press's Opus series). Occasionally its judgments are more decisive than the evidence upholding them, but it can be commended to all those seeking an introduction. **661** is more limited in several respects. It concentrates on a few key questions – urban demography, occupational structure, migration patterns – on one key area, Norfolk, and it is rather tight-lipped in its theorising. It says nothing about the urban cultural renaissance or about the 'political' and administrative structures of towns. It is very much a book by and for geographers. **662–3** are collections of essays, of which **662** is the most useful (not least in that it reprints the best articles of **663**! See also **717–24**, and key articles in **50** and **51**.

**664.** *English urban history 1500–1870* (4 vols., 1977–8)

A series of sixteen essays in four volumes produced for an Open University course, but perfectly usable by themselves. The first group is entitled 'the urban setting'; the second, 'the fabric of the traditional community'; the third, 'the traditional community under stress'; and the fourth, 'the use of the new urban community'.

## Social Problems and Policy

**665.** E. M. Leonard, *An early history of English poor relief* (1900)

**666.** G. Oxley, *Poor relief in England and Wales, 1601–1834* (1974)

**667.** G. Taylor, *The problem of poverty, 1660–1834* (1969)

**668.** E. M. Hampson, *the treatment of poverty in Cambridgeshire, 1597–1834* (1934)

**665** is a very dry-as-dust exegesis of the Tudor and Stuart poor laws, most remarkable today for its assertion that 'never, since the 1630s, has there been so much provision for the able-bodied poor'. On the eve of the Lloyd George budget of 1909 this could still be said. **666** is a most useful guide to the variegated experience of different regions and parishes under the old poor law. Lucid, firm and brisk, it is both an excellent introduction to the problems of poor law administration and a guide to those who might like to undertake a little local research project of their own. **667** is in Longman's Seminar Studies series and is another straightforward account. **668** is neatly and clearly laid out with separate treatment of the city of Cambridge, of the shire, and of Wisbech in the first half of the seventeenth century, and a general chapter on the implementation of the settlement laws in the later part of the century (for which see also articles **X391–2**).

**669.** W. K. Jordan, *Philanthropy in England, 1480–1660* (1959)

**670.** W. K. Jordan, *The charities of London, 1480–1660* (1960)

**671.** W. K. Jordan, *The charities of rural England, 1480–1660* (1961)

**672.** G. Jones, *History of the law of charity, 1532–1827* (1969)

It is Jordan's contention that charitable bequests bore the brunt of alleviating the lot of the poor. **669–71** are parallel volumes looking at different aspects of the problem. By analysing all extant wills for ten counties between 1480 and 1660, he sought to display (in **669**) the social and geographical origins of benefactors, to discuss the varied ends to which their bequests were directed, and to examine changes over time. In **670** he examined the effects of these bequests in London, in **671** their effects in Buckinghamshire, Norfolk and Yorkshire. He ignored problems of inflation, and was very loose in his use of social and religious labels, so that much of his work is vitiated. The three volumes were reviewed in successive years (1960–2) in *Economic History Review* by Professors Coleman, Trevor-Roper, and Aylmer and make excellent and contrasted reading. A number of subordinate county studies were produced by Jordan for county record society volumes. **672** is an important addition with its treatment of the work of seventeenth-century commissioners for charitable uses.

**673.** J. W. Willis-Bund (ed.), *Worcestershire quarter sessions rolls, 1591–1643* (1900)

**674.** S. A. Peyton (ed.), 'Lincolnshire quarter sessions minutes' *Lincolnshire Record Society*, vol. 25 (1931)

**675.** J. S. Cockburn (ed.), *Crime in England, 1550–1800* (1977)

The history of crime is a new subject. The raw materials of prosecutions for treasons, felonies and misdemeanours have been made available for many counties (see appendix 3 in **5**). **673–4** are two volumes with long and detailed introductions on procedure and the incidence of prosecutions. **72** offers a guide to prosecutions at assizes, and **73–4** and article **X357** are also relevant. More recently, historians have tried to approach the subject sociologically. The result is a spate of articles of varying sophistication which all seem to me to assume that there is some rough-and-ready relationship between the incidence of prosecutions and the incidence of 'crime' (itself a concept alien to the period). The introduction by G. R. Elton to **675**, indeed, points out the hazards that other contributors to that volume do not heed. Nonetheless **675** represents a great step forward, and the general level of sensitivity to the evidential problems, if not the conceptual ones, is quite high. The chapters by J. Baker on procedure at common law, J. S. Cockburn on the nature and incidence of crime and M. Ingram on law and disorder in Wiltshire are particularly good, and there is much of interest in the articles of J. Sharpe and T. Curtis on Essex and Cheshire.

**676.** M. Beloff, *Public order and popular disturbance, 1660–1714* (1938)

**677.** J. Brewer and J. Styles (eds.), *An ungovernable people* (1980)

It is astonishing that **676** is still the only full book in its field. The chapter headings reveal its slant: after general chapters on the social and political background, they are 'the food supply', 'agriculture and industry', 'the fiscal system and recoinage', 'the army and the navy and the people', 'popular disturbances and the machinery of the state'. There is, however, an increasingly large article literature on the subject, much of it deriving from the work of eighteenth- and nineteenth-century historians, notably E. P. Thompson. The treatment of riot as a rational and disciplined response to the abuse of power by agencies of social control is now well-established. **677** represents the best work achieved for our period using or reacting to that model. J. Walter writes on the Malden grain riots in early seventeenth-century Essex; K. Wrightson contrasts the views of magistrates and parish officers in seventeenth-century Essex and Lancashire; R. Malcolmson on the Kingswood riots near Bristol which begin in 1709. The other chapters deal with the eighteenth century.

**678.** M. James, *Social problems and policy in the puritan revolution* (1930)

**679.** M. G. Davies, *The enforcement of English apprenticeship, 1563–1642* (1956)

**680.** N. S. B. Gras, *The evolution of the English corn laws* (1915)

**681.** W. Minchinton (ed.), *Wage regulation in pre-industrial England* (1972)

**678** is an important book straining too hard to find a fundamental shift in economic and social thought and action during the English Revolution. It is based overwhelmingly on the pamphlet literature of the time and looks at the impact of the civil war on the economy, at the problems of the land, industrial regulation, poor relief, social utopianism and at democratic aspirations of the Guilds and in the City of London. Read it alongside **787**. **679** is a model of careful and intelligent scholarship and looks at the bold aims and limited success of the Statute of Artificers of 1563. It is at its best on the work of private informers and patentees who did far more than the J.P.s and other public agencies (though still too little). **680** treats the period down to 1689 and looks at the regulation of the marketing of grain by the crown and by local governors. **681** reprints works by Kelsall and Tawney on wage-fixing by J.P.s under the statute of 1563, together with a good introduction by the editor bringing the material up-to-date (though curiously it ignores the work of Bindoff on the 1563 statute).

**682.** K. V. Thomas, *Religion and the decline of magic* (1971)

**683.** A. Macfarlane, *Witchcraft in Tudor and Stuart England* (1970)

**684.** B. Capp, *Astrology and the popular press* (1979)

**682** is one of the great books of recent years, an immensely widely researched, subtly argued and broadly conceived study of the mental world of the common people and others in early modern England. It examines the impact of the Reformation on the beliefs of the people at large and penetrates the unfamiliar world of superstition, magic and witchcraft. It argues that the protestant Reformation, with its discouragement of ritual and set formulae lending themselves to popular magical and counter-magical explanations, left a vacuum which was filled by increasing recourse to wizards, cunning men and women, etc. Some have found the myriad examples wearing, but most have delighted in the richness of texture and the sensitive use of insights from anthropology which have provided Thomas with some of his questions, but not with his answers. Much the same goes for **683**, which looks at one aspect of the problem for one county (Essex) in the hundred years after 1560 and finds the key to witchcraft prosecutions to lie in the sense of guilt in the victim at his failure to behave in a neighbourly fashion towards a poor, usually elderly, female. **682** has something to say about astrology, but this subject is now at a centre of a long and important study of almanacs which covers the period 1500–1800 (**684**). 'Apart from the Bible, almanacs were the most influential and widely dispersed form of literature', selling 400,000 copies a year by the late seventeenth century. Apart from their astrological uses, almanacs are an important source for establishing conventional wisdoms of the period about a host of subjects – the weather, leisure, agriculture, disease, sex. This is an important work.

## Education

**685.** D. Cressy, *Education in Tudor and Stuart England* (1975)

**686.** J. Lawson and H. Silver, *A social history of education in England* (1973)

**685** is a reader drawing on a wide range of sixteenth- and seventeenth-century authors to present a clear account of developments both in schools and universities. In general I prefer to start people off with it rather than with **686**, a clearly laid-out, judicious but rather dull textbook that devotes some 130 pages to every aspect of early modern education.

**687.** M. Curtis, *Oxford and Cambridge in transition* (1959)

**688.** H. F. Kearney, *Scholars and gentlemen, 1500–1700* (1970)

**689.** L. Stone (ed.), *The university in society* (vol. I, 1974)

**687** covers the century down to 1640 and offers a cogent interpretation of changes in the size and composition of the student body, in the relationship of colleges, halls and university, and of developments in the formal and informal curriculum. **688** is much slighter, and looks both at the changing social function of the universities and also at the formal curriculum. **689** is a collection of essays, of which the editor's own on the size and composition of the student body at Oxford is convincing (despite some cavalier handling of the evidence), and V. Morgan's on the complex relationship between particular colleges and particular regions is richly suggestive. Stone's two articles on literacy and the educational revolution are amongst his best works (**X388** and **X390**). Oxford University Press has in hand a multi-volume history of its university, and the seventeenth-century volume, edited by H. R. Trevor-Roper, is well advanced.

**690.** W. A. L. Vincent, *The state and school education in England, 1640–1660* (1950)

**691.** W. A. L. Vincent, *The English grammar school, 1660–1714* (1969)

**692.** M. G. Jones, *The charity school movement* (1938)

**693.** B. Simon (ed.), *Education in Leicestershire, 1540–1940* (1968)

**690** is a history of the *debate about* education and is built around the pamphlet literature inspired by Hartlib, Dury, Comenius and Sir William Petty. It also looks at the sponsorship by both Long Parliament and Lord Protector of schools and universities and at the anti-intellectual wing of puritanism. It contains a useful list of all endowed grammar schools in existence between 1600 and 1660. **691** concentrates on the schools, and (after a brief introduction on the number and distribution) on the 'daily round', 'the demand and need for reform' and on the lot of the schoolmasters. It is a pleasant, rather undemanding book. **692** is a thorough history of elementary education in England, Scotland, Ireland and Wales. Although it is mainly concerned with the eighteenth century, it contains an important study of the origins and developments of the Society for Promoting Christian Knowledge. That body has more recently published many of the books discussed here, particularly in chapter 6. **693** is a collection of useful essays, but for the best approach to the local history of English schools, see the *Victorian County Histories*. The chapters on education usually form part of the first or second volume for each county.

# 9
# LOCAL STUDIES

Local history has always been a strong and marked feature in the historiography of early modern England. The mid-nineteenth century witnessed the foundation of archaeological and historical societies in most counties, many of them with branches devoted to the publication of county records. The period 1890–1920 saw a fresh surge of activity in two particular areas – the publication of local histories of the civil war period and the systematic publication of the earliest quarter sessions order books or mainprise files, in most cases dating from the late sixteenth or early seventeenth century. The fruits of these endeavours can be readily traced in the bibliographies of Davies and Keeler or of Aylmer and Morrill (**1**, **5**). It must be said, however, that the resulting works were fundamentally antiquarian rather than historical: they described how things were, but they did not seek to explain why they happened as they did. Furthermore, they assumed that the political and religious attitudes which Gardiner and others had proclaimed as the 'national' pattern underlay the actions of the leaders of each region.

The local histories which have appeared in the past twenty years are not simply a continuation or revival of these traditions but represent a radical new departure. Although the creation of new county record offices in the inter-war years was no doubt a stimulus, it is not the main reason for this breakthrough. One obvious reason for the boom in local history is the rise of the Ph.D. industry. A county study based on a relatively discreet and manageable body of manuscripts often on the doorstep of the universities makes an obvious thesis project. Another spur to seventeenth-century local history was the state of civil war studies in the mid-1950s. This was the age of the 'storm over the gentry' (e.g. **653–5**), with historians committed to theorising rather wildly around socially-determinist models. Their generalisations cried out for detailed local studies. Historians like Cliffe (**703**) and Blackwood (**704**) were expressly inspired by that challenge. But what turned local studies from a subsidiary into a major branch of early modern historiography was the extraordinarily perceptive and imaginative work of two historians, Professors Barnes and Everitt, whose studies of pre-civil war Somerset and civil war Kent have formed the basis of a new genre. (For their particular contributions see below **705**, **709**).

The new tradition has been built upon the following arguments: (*a*) That the social, institutional and political arrangements in most counties by 1600 were so distinctive, inward-looking and semi-autonomous that they require to be treated separately. England at this period is more like a federated state than a unitary national state. (*b*) Effective control over the social, political and (to a lesser extent) religious institutions of each county lay with a fairly self-evident and largely self-sustaining group of gentry families, distinguished from the rest of the community by their wealth, by their interconnections of blood and marriage, by a distinctive educational background. The crown at any moment chose the actual governors from among the very restricted number of families making up these *county communities*. (*c*) The crown could only govern (in particular, could only raise money, enforce its social and economic policies, maintain law and order) through establishing an identity of interest with these county governors. This meant operating an elaborate system of quid-pro-quos, itself a combination of sticks and carrots. It has been argued by local historians that the early Stuarts failed to operate this system as skilfully as Elizabeth I had done. Most have preferred to see this as a lack of skill on the crown's part rather than the collapse of the system itself from wider forces. (*d*) National issues did not impinge as directly on provincial squires and others as historians have assumed. Rather, national issues took on different resonances in each local context and became intricately bound up with purely local issues and groupings.

Local studies have thus tended to emphasise the uniqueness of each county's response to the crises of the mid-seventeenth century and have also found that much parliamentarianism grew out of an experience of centralist encroachment, and was deeply conservative in nature. They have also tended to emphasise the extent of neutralism both in 1642 and 1645–6. There are a signs of a backlash against these last findings, and Professor Clive Holmes has challenged the central notion of a 'county community' in a review of **695** in the *American Historical Review* (1978). A further reaction can be predicted and a healthy debate should ensue. However, a London-and-Westminister-based account of the civil war will never again be possible. Already, the extent to which electoral and parliamentary history has been rewritten in the light of the new county histories can be seen in such works as **12** and **135** – which take up localism without capitulating to it. No seventeenth-century local study has yet got the symbiotic relationship between centre and provinces right. For a model of how this can be achieved, see A. Hassell Smith, *County and court: government and politics in Elizabethan Norfolk* (1974). Those who see below that I am myself an exponent of this school may suspect the above to be unduly complaisant. So let me emphasise how limited the 'localist' thought has been. Most of the studies published (and they represent a tithe of the Ph.D. theses completed in this field) concern themselves overwhelmingly with the government of particular shires before or during the civil war or with the study of civil war allegiances. At least four areas of equal significance have been barely touched: (*a*) Ecclesiastical history has been subsumed within several of these studies, but never satisfactorily. There is nothing to compare with the books of C. Haigh (*Reformation and resistance in Tudor Lancashire* (1972)) or R. B. Manning (*Religion and society in Elizabethan Sussex* (1967)). (*b*) Large urban communities were more autonomous than were the shires. Yet the only study to appear on a similar scale is Howell's on Newcastle-upon-Tyne (**724**). (*c*) Local studies have remained for the most part studies of the gentry, often of the greater gentry. Local studies have made far too little attempt to penetrate more deeply to explore the political behaviour and beliefs of other social groups. (*d*) Most surprising of all, local studies have been concentrated in the period up to 1660. The Restoration and post-Revolution periods cry out for similar treatment, but have not received it. Local historians have a lot to answer for as well as a lot to take credit for. There is much still to be done.

**694.** P. Clark, *English provincial society from the Reformation to the Revolution: religion, politics and society in Kent, 1500–1640* (1977)

**695.** A. Fletcher, *A county community in peace and war: Sussex, 1600–1660* (1976)

**694** is an immense and broadly conceived work. It attempts to describe the changing economic and social structure of Kent and to relate these changes to developments in the political, social, religious and legal institutions of the county. It also seeks to describe the changing relationships between national and local institutions. Chapters 9–12 relate directly to the period 1603–40, while chapter 13 follows up many of the book's themes, though more impressionistically, to 1720. The narrative often appears to proceed further than the evidence should permit, and the argument is sometimes over-schematic, but the effort of trying to relate 'the many faces of provincial life' is frequently very rewarding. Urban history is particularly well woven into the book. **695** is much more carefully researched, much more clearly written, but much more exclusively concerned with the gentry alone. It lacks the breadth of **694**, but is exceptionally clear on religion, and on political and administrative developments before and during the civil war. It is now the best introduction to advanced students of what a 'county study' can do to enhance our general understanding of the period.

**696.** C. H. Chalkin, *Seventeenth-century Kent* (1965)

**697.** C. M. Bouch and G. P. Jones, *The Lakeland counties, 1500–1830* (1961)

**698.** M. James, *Family, lineage and civil society: a study of society, politics and mentality in the Durham region, 1500–1640* (1974)

**699.** S. J. and S. J. Watts, *From border to middle shire: Northumberland, 1586–1625* (1975)

**696** is an attractive and clear account of Kentish society and economy in the seventeenth century and of the changes occurring there (agricultural diversification and intensification, the decline of the Wealden cloth trade and the rise of shipbuilding and allied trade in the north). There are sections on topography, demography, farming, industry and trade and social organisation. Only the demographic section would require serious revision. **697** tells a similar story – though the changes occur later – for Cumberland and Westmorland and is particularly good on the survival of the manorial system. It needs to be supplemented now by the work of J. V. Beckett (articles **X6, X348**). **698** is a much more complex book. Once again it is chronicling a movement away from a 'traditional' economy to a market economy – though this development is very thinly etched here – but is mainly concerned with the emergence of new social and political institutions appropriate to the new economic values – a 'civil society' in which the extended kinship network and noble household are replaced by a more fissiparous structure. This in turn is seen to have implications for political values and practice. Some of the assumptions are rather simplistic, but the argument itself is subtle and persuasive. **699** takes us even further north and looks at the changes in politics wrought by demographic and economic change and by the accession of James VI to the throne of England, with its resultant easing of border tensions. Unfortunately the authors' approach is a largely narrative one and I regret to say I found it opaque and too detailed.

**700.** M. Spufford, *Contrasting communities* (1974)

**701.** D. Hey, *An English rural community: Myddle under the Tudors and Stuarts* (1974)

**702.** W. G. Hoskins. *The Midland peasant* (1957)

**700** is a brilliant book which looks at the economic, educational and religious life of three Cambridgeshire communities sharply contrasted in their topography, structure and values; Chippenham lies in the chalk lands of east Cambridgeshire, Orwell on the clay of west Cambridgeshire, and Willingham in the northern fens. The different fate of the small landholders in each, and the explanations offered, are of the greatest possible interest and importance. **701** looks at a single community in Shropshire for which we have a unique source: a detailed commentary by a late-seventeenth-century vicar of the history and circumstances of the members of his parish. Hey's study is a wide-ranging one – topography, demography, economic, social and employment structures, mobility, and the 'mental world'. More could have been squeezed from the sources, but the picture is well-rounded and very readable. **702** looks at the economic and social changes in Wigston Magna (Leicestershire) between 1066 and 1900. There is a chapter specifically on 'peasant society, 1600–1766' and much of the material in the surrounding chapters is relevant. See also **A12** (p. 179).

**703.** J. T. Cliffe, *The Yorkshire gentry from the Reformation to the civil war* (1969)

**704.** B. G. Blackwood, *The Lancashire gentry and the Great Rebellion* (1978)

**703** sets out to resolve the 'gentry controversy' by establishing whether the royalist gentry were declining and the parliamentarians rising, or vice versa. It turned out that neither was the case (or else that both were), but a great deal of important information about the fortunes, aspirations and variety of experience of the gentry is revealed by the book. The chapters on government and administration are less satisfactory, and some of the sources used to calculate wealth have been quite successfully attacked as unreliable. **704** takes the story of the Lancashire gentry down to 1700. It is a group profile, based on a large number of tables and it is in four sections: the Lancashire gentry on the eve of the civil war; cavalier and roundhead gentry, and the differences between them as groups; the roundheads in power, and their failure to prosper in the long term; the royalists in defeat, and their ability to survive the experience and to bounce back at the Restoration.

**705.** T. G. Barnes, *Somerset, 1625–1642* (1961)

**706.** W. B. Willcox, *Gloucestershire, 1590–1640* (1940)

**707.** J. S. Morrill, *The Cheshire Grand Jury 1625–1659* (1975)

**708.** T. G. Barnes, *The clerk of the peace in Caroline Somerset* (1961)

**705** is a very important study of the institutions of a county stretched to the limit and collapsing under the strain of the demands imposed by Charles I. Its integration of a 'political' dimension in the shape of Sir Robert Phelips' rivalry with Lord Poulet and Sir John Stawell is brilliantly handled. This is a very important book, the ramifications of which are very broad. It certainly makes **706**, a thorough and workmanlike survey of all the institutions of Gloucestershire, seem very dull. **707–8** are 18,000–20,000 word essays in Leicester University Press's Occasional Papers in Local History series and their titles speak for themselves. **707** is subtitled 'a social and administrative study'.

**709.** A. M. Everitt, *The community of Kent and the Great Rebellion* (1966)

**710.** A. M. Everitt, *Suffolk in the Great Rebellion* (1960)

**711.** J. S. Morrill, *Cheshire, 1630–1660* (1974)

**712.** D. E. Underdown, *Somerset in the civil wars and interregnum* (1973)

**713.** E. A. Andriette, *Devon and Exeter in the civil war* (1972)

**714.** R. W. Ketton-Cremer, *Norfolk in the civil war* (1969)

**715.** A. C. Wood, *Nottinghamshire in the civil wars* (1934)

**716.** M. Coate, *Cornwall in the great civil war and interregnum* (1940)

**709** is the trail-blazer here, a most stimulating account of the way the peculiar characteristics of Kentish society and institutions shaped the response of the county to the civil war. It shows both how far purely local issues contributed to men's political decisions, and the extent to which the efforts of parliament to centralise, and of local radicals to reform, the institutions of the county, remained at the centre of the struggle for the county. **710** is a collection of texts with an eighty-page introduction finding the same perspective producing distinctively different patterns in Suffolk. **711–12** both follow the same general line, but modify Everitt's model. **711** (a revised doctoral thesis) is more fully researched, devotes more space to the period after the civil wars and is less exclusively concerned about the gentry, but is far too myopic about the events of 1640–2: there is a serious error of perspective. **712** is shrewder and clearer and has an excellent section on the effects of war-weariness in the late 1640s. The other books are of less general interest. They illuminate the history of their chosen shires rather than the history of England. **713** is conceptually the weakest and the least well written; **714** is marvellous on family history and on the nuances of political behaviour, suspect on ideology; **715** is a fine, clear narrative of events, **716** simply an excellent all-round account. The chapter on religion stands up particularly well.

**717.** W. Brett-James, *The growth of Stuart England* (1935)

**718.** T. F. Reddaway, *The rebuilding of London* (1940)

**717** is a long, rather antiquarian work in the form of a series of essays (partly chronological, partly topographical) very much concerned with the visual and architectural aspects of the subject. **718** is a clear, absorbing and skilful account of the administrative, financial, architectural and social problems which followed the Great Fire in 1666. There was also a constitutional dimension which is not fully treated here. See also **153–4**.

**719.** A. Dyer, *The city of Worcester in the sixteenth century* (1973)

**720.** W. MacCaffrey, *Exeter, 1540–1640* (1958)

**721.** W. B. Stephens, *Seventeenth-century Exeter* (1958)

**722.** Sir J. Hill, *Tudor and Stuart Lincoln* (1956)

**723.** C. N. Parkinson, *The rise of the port of Liverpool* (1952)

Much of the evidence for **719** is drawn from the early seventeenth century. It looks at the demography, economy, social organisation, government and religion of the town, and is particularly good on Worcester's relationship with its hinterland. **720** is equally wide-ranging but is stronger on the government of the city than on its economy. It thus neatly complements **721** which is a purely economic study, though an important one, since it chronicles the transformation of the west-country cloth industry and its impact on patterns of trade. **722** is a less inquisitive and less well researched general account of a declining county town, while **723** is the 'history of a seaport and not of a city' down to 1793. It thus concentrates on the decline of the Irish trade and the rise of the Atlantic trades to the exclusion of Liverpool's own industrial base. For a number of useful articles see the *Urban History Yearbook* (annually since 1974).

**724.** R. Howell, *Newcastle-upon-Tyne in the puritan revolution* (1967)

**724** is the only study of urban politics (other than on London). It finds a preoccupation with local issues and political prudentialism at least as marked in the Newcastle area as county historians have found it in the shires, and it finds the effects of a parliamentarian victory surprisingly limited.

**725.** P. Styles, *Studies in seventeenth-century West Midlands history* (1978)

The collected papers of the distinguished historian and antiquarian, published posthumously. The author wrote austerely and found it hard to generalise, but several of these essays are of very wide interest. All are impeccably researched and are grounded in a remarkable topographical and genealogical knowledge. Political historians should all get to know 'the City of Worcester during the civil wars' and 'the corporation of Bewdley under the late Stuarts', while social historians should already recognise as basic texts 'the social structure of Kineton hundred in the reign of Charles II' and 'the heralds' visitation of Warwickshire 1682–3'. There are nine essays altogether.

# 10
# CULTURAL HISTORY

The problems of selection here have been particularly acute, partly because of my own comparative lack of expertise, and partly because so little has been written by trained historians, so much by others. It is a curious fact about advanced education in England (and to a lesser extent in Scotland) that while we have tried, particularly in the new universities, to create less restricted unilinear courses, the result has been multi-disciplinary rather than inter-disciplinary teaching. This may be less true than it was, but there has been really very little sign yet that scholars are emerging who are capable of fusing elements of historical and literary methodology. At any rate, most books on the arts are written by non-historians, and while some of the very many ways literature scholars go about their work involve a close study of the social and political context within which literature is produced, it must be said that their attempts to characterise such contexts have not been very sophisticated. Of course the reverse is also true: few historians write about literature in ways that are felt to be sensitive or intelligent by English scholars (though there are exceptions, of whom Christopher Hill is the clearest example). This is not intended to be critical comment, simply a demonstration of the problems of truly inter-disciplinary work, problems which for largely practical reasons seem to have been ironed out between historians and social scientists or historians and natural scientists, but not yet between historians and the pure arts specialists. What follows is therefore a rather haphazard collection.

The pool of books from which selections had to be made was enormous, and I did no more than take the advice of others in constructing a short list and then browsing within that, excluding those things which – however interesting – seemed to me to be of no immediate interest to those trying to understand the mental world or social history of seventeenth-century England. It transpired that there was a great deal of value on the theatre, far less on poetry or prose (though books on two key poets, Milton and Dryden, appear elsewhere in chapter 3). I looked in vain (but perhaps in the wrong places) for work on why people wrote poetry, and who for. On the visual arts and music, I found fewer books, but those which were relevant were of more immediate value to historians and included the only book which seemed to me a serious work of cultural history (**761**). When I came to consider the history of science, the situation was very different. Here there is a great deal of excellent work, clear, intelligent and incisive. The great issue for historians of science – as for all historians of ideas, though the former appear to have formulated it more decisively – is whether their subject is an exercise in the genealogy of ideas or whether it is an aspect of social history, an attempt to rationalise and make sense of knowledge of the 'natural world' in terms which harmonise with men's conception of themselves, their society and their political and religious institutions. Much of the writing about particular scientific problems addresses itself to this question, and there has been a tendency for books to move to one side or other of the divide, rather than to attempt to straddle it. I found the whole debate illuminating and invigorating rather than (as so often with such wrangles) obfuscatory.

## Literature and the Press

**726.** B. Ford (ed.), *The Pelican guide to English literature*, vols. 2–4 (1955, 1956, 1957)

**727.** C. Ricks (ed.), *Sphere history of literature in the English language*, vols. 2–3 (1970–1)

These are alternative introductory surveys to the literature of the period written by English scholars and directed at English students or the general reader, but both are quite successful in relating the works discussed to their historical context. The first of four stated objectives of **726** is 'to provide an account of the social context of literature in each period, attempting to answer such questions as "why did the literature of this period deal with this rather than that kind of question"', and each volume has an interesting opening essay on the social background. Volume 2 covers 1558–1625 (*The age of Shakespeare*), volume 3 1625–*c.* 1670 (*From Donne to Marvell*), volume 4 *c.* 1660–1780 (*From Dryden to Johnson*). **727** likewise aims 'to give a modern reader a sense of the many contexts within which literature exists'. Volume 2 (*English poetry and prose, 1540–1640*) has separate chapters on particular authors and genres, with a final chapter on the development of prose style during the period; volume 3 (*English drama down to*

*1710*) is similar. In general I found **727** crisper, less donnish than **726** and on some subjects played down in **726** (e.g. Milton and Restoration comedy) far better.

**728.** B. Willey, *The seventeenth-century background* (1934)

**729.** C. V. Wedgwood, *Seventeenth-century English literature* (1950, 1976)

**730.** S. L. Bethell, *The cultural revolution of the seventeenth century* (1952)

**731.** C. V. Wedgwood, *Poetry and politics under the Stuarts* (1960)

**728** is a classic which was and is intended to introduce the English student and the general reader to the theological and philosophical traditions within which poets and playwrights worked. It is most successful as such. See particularly the essays on Bacon, on Hobbes and on the Cambridge Platonists. **729** is more flowery and rhetorical, but the argument – that the century saw the triumph of the English language as a literary medium – is clearly and vigorously argued. **730** is a study of the relationship between theology and literature, arguing that developments in the former affected the latter in the seventeenth century. It examines the treatment of faith and reason, and the replacement of the 'chain of being' cosmology by one derived from natural philosophy, and looks for the appropriate changes in literary theory and practice. **731** is a lightweight but clear and often surprising study of the ways writers reacted to the political upheavals of the seventeenth century.

**732.** L. C. Knights, *Drama and society in the age of Jonson* (1937)

**733.** M. C. Bradbrook, *The living monument* (1976)

**732** was an astonishingly pioneering work in its day – an attempt to dispel 'the exasperating haziness of all those who have attempted to make some correlation between economic activities and culture'. The reliance upon Tawney and Weber will seem less acceptable to most readers nowadays than it did in 1937, but there is still much that is stimulating in it. **733** is far more subtle in its rather different task of analysing 'the sociology of the theatre', a book which contains important studies on Shakespeare's treatment of history, on the structure of Tudor and early Stuart society, on Jonson's court masques, and on the variety and range of theatrical venues in Jacobean London.

**734.** A. Gurr, *The Shakespearean stage, 1574–1642* (1970)

**735.** A. Harbage, *Shakespeare's audience* (1970)

**736.** G. E. Bentley (ed.), *The seventeenth-century stage* (1968)

Three similar books: **734** is a brisk and thorough account of the companies, players, playhouses, staging and audiences of the period; **735** is an unadorned, unpretentious book with practical chapter heads like 'the evidence' (which turns out to be extensive) 'how many people?' 'what kind of people?' 'behaviour', etc. **736** is a collection of essays concerned with actors, acting, theatres and productions. Much of it is concerned with technical questions, but others are of interest to social historians.

**737.** E. Welsford, *The court masque* (1928)

**738.** S. Orgel, *The Jonsonian masque* (1967)

**739.** S. Orgel, *The illusion of power* (1975)

**740.** J. G. Demaray, *Milton and the masque* (1968)

**737** is still the basic guide to the masque, though it is mainly concerned with the pre-Stuart period. Its emphasis is on the relationship between the masques and other art-forms. **738–9** are complementary works. Jonson said that masques 'either have been or ought to be mirrors of man's life', and **738** studies six of his masques to demonstrate how he tried to combine spectacle, allegory and art-form. **739** looks at Charles I's use of theatre to evoke and symbolise his preoccupation with order, harmony and purity. Given the success of his self-mystification, the book could as easily have been titled 'the power of illusion'. **740** is a short, clear account of the masques of the 1630s and of the context within which Milton's *Comus* came to be conceived and performed. For other works on Milton, see **221–4**. For the masques, see also **12** and **149**.

**741.** A. Nicholl, *Restoration drama (1660–1700)* (1928, 1940)

**742.** R. D Hume, *The development of English drama in the late seventeenth century* (1976)

**741** is a thorough and down-to-earth work which looks at the theatre (audience, appearance, personnel) and at cultural influences, domestic and foreign, which shaped tragedy and comedy in the period. It contains useful appendices on the location, number and regulation of theatres. **742** is a much more analytical and probing work, concentrating on one aspect of the problem – changes in theatrical fashion over the period 1660–1710. Most relevant to historians are the chapters on 'theatres and audiences' and on the 'political dramas' of the 1680s.

**743.** R. C. Bald, *John Donne: a life* (1970)

**744.** D. Parker, *John Donne and his world* (1975)

**743** is a comprehensive, detailed and broadly conceived life in narrative form. **744** is much slighter, but is a well-illustrated life and times, pleasant and with a good discussion of cultural patronage.

**745.** E. N. S. Thompson, *The controversy between the puritans and the stage* (1903)

**746.** R. Fraser, *The war against poetry* (1970)

**745** is still the fullest treatment of this theme, though a major new assessment by M. Heinemann is imminent. **745** deals with the chronology of the attacks and with the arguments put forward on both sides. Only half of it is concerned with our period. **746** is a study of the attack by 'protestants' on secular verse in the sixteenth and seventeenth centuries. It too examines the arguments used and traces their intellectual lineage.

**747.** I. Rivers, *The poetry of conservatism* (1973)

**747** is a 'study of poets and public affairs from Jonson to Pope' (i.e. 1600–1745). The key figures are Jonson, Milton, Marvell, Dryden and Pope, and the book looks at 'public poetry, its context, its intentions, its uses, and its limitations'. Its notion of 'conservative' appears to be a rather perverse one. For Milton, see also **221–4**, and for Marvell, see also **249**.

**748.** M. Hunter, *John Aubrey and the realm of learning* (1975)

**749.** R. T. Peterson, *Sir Kenelm Digby* (1956)

**750.** C. H. Josten, *Elias Ashmole* (1958)

These are studies of some of the great virtuosi of the century. **748** is an intellectual biography of the author of *Brief Lives*, one of the most versatile men of his age. It pays particular attention to his scientific and antiquarian interests. It is a model study of its kind. **749** is a chronological account of an even more formidable man. It is less readable, but with a man hailed as 'the ornament of England' whose name appears everywhere – 'in contemporary letters and records, in works on navigation, Catholicism, medicine, court life, privateering, embryology, book collecting, botany, mathematics, cookery' – it can still astonish. **750** rather overdoes a good thing. It is a huge, formless, antiquarian life of Ashmole concentrating on his daily life as astrologer, necromancer, alchemist and archivist as prelude to four other volumes of his works, and it misses the neo-platonism which is the organising principle in his life.

**751.** P. Earle, *The world of Defoe* (1976)

**752.** P. Rogers, *The Augustan vision* (1974)

**753.** P. Rogers, *Grub Street* (1972)

**754.** M. M. Foot, *The pen and the sword* (1957)

**751** falls into four parts: a biography of Defoe; a discussion of his beliefs and values; an account of the economy and society he chronicled; and an account of the life cycle of individuals of the time. It is clear and readable but not particularly penetrating. **752** is a more ambitious and interesting attempt to relate literary work to the cultural and social aspirations of the elite of Defoe's time. It seeks to 'call out our sympathy and identification with the exuberance and energy of the age'. **753**, by the same author, is an excellent study which aims 'to show how the Augustan Satirists built upon the facts of contemporary life'. **754** looks at one of Grub Street's triumphs. It is a dramatic account of the literary assassination of the Duke of Marlborough by Jonathan Swift in 1709–10.

**755.** G. A. Cranfield, *The press and society* (1978)

**756.** M. Plant, *The English book trade* (1939)

**757.** H. Bennett, *English books and readers, 1603–1640* (1970)

**758.** J. Frank, *The beginnings of the English newspaper* (1961)

**759.** F. S. Siebert, *The freedom of the press* (1952)

**760.** D. Foxon, *Libertine literature in England, 1660–1745* (1964)

**755** is a clear introduction to its subject, covering 1476–1976, but it devotes only forty pages to our period and does little more than summarise **756–60**. **756** also covers 500 years, but devotes 260 pages to the sixteenth to eighteenth centuries. It is divided topically (the demand for books / the division of labour within the industry / the structure of the industry during the period of hand production / copyright problems / the supply of paper and binding materials / prices / size of editions, etc). **757** is the third and final volume of a work which also began with Caxton. The first part looks at publishing – at printing, regulations of the trade, translations and pirate editions, etc. The second – and larger – part, surveys the literature published during these forty years under ten main heads (religion / law / educational treatises, etc.), and the final chapter looks at the marketing of books. **758** examines one crucial development of the century. It offers a strictly chronological account of the volume, content and control of news books. All but nineteen pages concern the period 1642–60. **759** is an important (if rather dry) study of the theory and practice of government regulations of printing. It devotes 200 pages to the seventeenth century in three chronological sections. **760** is a very brief work most useful for its brisk account of all the legal actions against allegedly obscene publications.

### The Visual Arts

**761.** J. Hook, *The baroque age in England* (1976)

**762.** M. Foss, *The age of patronage* (1971)

**761** is an outstanding attempt to relate cultural history to its socio-economic matrix. It assesses the English baroque (concentrating on the seventy-five years after 1660) by looking at the political framework, at the status of the artist, at the nature of patronage, at money and materials, and at aesthetic theorising within the period. There are sixty-six excellent black and white illustrations covering all the visual arts, and two appendices listing the 'creative elite' and 'an alphabetical list of some major Baroque architecture'. **762** is an attractive, lightweight alternative, certainly worth exploring if **761** is not to hand.

**763.** M. Whinney and O. Millar, *English art, 1625–1714* (1957)

**764.** J. Summerson, *Architecture in Britain, 1530–1830* (1953)

**765.** K. Downes, *English baroque architecture* (1966)

These are all books concerned more with the genealogy of styles and influences than with the social history of art, but all are clear and well illustrated. **763** looks at painting, sculpture, architecture, tapestry-work, etc. **764** is more purely descriptive and covers only fairly grand building projects, whereas **765** looks at the diffusion of the ideas behind the grand designs into the more modest building of town-houses, inns, etc. It does not altogether fulfil its promise to demonstrate that 'rigid sociological theories of culture are apt to be upset by the fact that cultural events happen first'.

**766.** J. Summerson, *Inigo Jones* (1966)

**767.** J. Summerson, *Christopher Wren* (1963)

**768.** K. Downes, *Christopher Wren* (1971)

**769.** R. Dutton, *The Age of Wren* (1951)

**766–7** are straightforward accounts of the life and works of the two greatest architects of the century, most concerned to justify their reputation for aesthetic excellence. The same can be said of **768–9**, but **768** is fuller than its rivals on Wren's background and intellectual development.

**770.** D. M. Bergeron, *English civic pageantry, 1558–1642* (1971)
This looks, rather literally and chronologically, at Royal Progresses and Entries into London, at Lord Mayors' Shows and at Pageants. It is rather repetitive, and makes little attempt to explore the symbolism, but is full of lively detail.

## Music

**771.** P. le Huray, *Music and the Reformation in England, 1549–1660* (1959)

**772.** C. Dearnley, *English church music, 1660–1750* (1970)
Both these works are essentially musicological, but both have to deal with major ecclesiastical and liturgical change. **771** is more strictly chronological, and concentrates on the period before 1603, while **772** deals separately with court, cathedral and parochial music and seems fuller on the historical background.

**773.** W. L .Woodfill, *Musicians in English society from Elizabeth to Charles I* (1953)

**774.** J. Harley, *Music in Purcell's London* (1968)
**773** is a thorough survey of professional and amateur music-making, treating – in separate sections – the London companies, provincial professionals, church, court and amateurs. It is as much concerned with popular as with formal music. **774** has a similar prospectus (though confined to London) and although less well researched, I found it the livelier of the two. It would surely have benefited, however, from a more systematic analysis of patronage.

**775.** E. J. Dent, *Foundations of English opera* (1928)
This is still the best overall account, apparently, but it is concerned less with the social context than with the relationship between music and the theatre in general, and with the intrusion of continental, principally French, influences.

**776.** J. A. Westrup, *Purcell* (1937, 1975)
A straightforward, clear and balanced study, biographically and musicologically.

## Science

**777.** H. Butterfield, *Origins of modern science* (1957)

**778.** A. R. Hall, *Galileo to Newton, 1630–1720* (1963)

**779.** R. K. Merton, *Science, technology and society in seventeenth-century England* (1970)

**780.** R. S. Westfall, *Science and religion in seventeenth-century England* (1958, 1977)

**781.** G. N. Clark, *Science and social welfare in the age of Newton* (1949)

**782.** P. Mathias (ed.), *Science and society, 1600–1900* (1972)

**777** and **778** are excellent introductions, setting the English scientific revolution into a European context, and both, particularly **778**, studying the history of science as a branch of intellectual rather than social history. **779** treats it as the latter, describing itself as a 'work of historical sociology'. **777–9** are all overviews, syntheses, but **780** is meatier and longer, a major study of the interrelationships of scientific and religious thought, which finds the new insights in both spheres finally achieving a new harmony in the mind of Newton. **781** consists of four stimulating essays on the social history of science including a study of the relationship between economic incentive and invention, and on the social control of technological innovation. It draws freely on material from other centuries and countries. **782** contains three essays relevant to the seventeenth century – A. R. Hall on science, technology and utopias, P. M. Rattansi on the social interpretations of science and P. Mathias an 'who unbound Prometheus? science and technological change, 1600–1800'.

**783.** H. G. van Leeuwen, *The problem of certainty in English thought, 1630–1690* (1963)

**784.** R. H. Kargan, *Atomism in England from Hariot to Newton* (1966)

**783** is a study of how a solution was found to the philosophical problem of the certainty of knowledge. It looks at eight key authors' search for an answer: Bacon, Chillingworth, Tillotson, Wilkins, Glanvill, Boyle, Newton and Locke. It is brisk and clear. **784** is an exegesis of another key dogma of the scientific revolution: the view that all phenomena can be explained by matter and its motion.

**785.** P. Rossi, *Francis Bacon* (1968)

**786.** J. Stephens, *Francis Bacon and the style of science* (1975)

**785** is the translation of an Italian work first published in 1957. It is a study of Bacon's philosophy and philosophy of science. Its subtitle 'from magic to science' illustrates that Rossi shares others' awe in his subject. **786** is a study of Bacon's philosophical method and use of language. It is a rather technical work. For other books on Bacon, see **138–9**.

**787.** C. Webster, *The great instauration* (1975)

A long, diverse and important study of the great wave of reforming ideas and projects between 1626 and 1660 – the advancement of learning, the prolongation of life, man's dominion over nature. It examines scientific and medical ideas and practices and the formal and informal institutions which arose to control and extend them. The attempt to find common denominators in Baconianism and puritanism, and its eschewing of continental parallels and experience have been criticised, but it remains a magisterial survey and a delightful read.

**788.** M. Purver, *The Royal Society: concept and creation* (1967)

**789.** Sir H. Hartley, *The Royal Society, its origin and founders* (1960)

**790.** T. K. Hoppen, *The common scientist in the seventeenth century* (1970)

**788** proclaims itself as a revisionist work in finding the origins of the Royal Society at Oxford, derived from a refined Baconianism (freed from the vulgarised Baconianism of the Hartlib circle). The triumph of the Society is seen as the emancipation from all religious cosmologies. Others have found the case overstated, and where not overstated, less original than it claims to be, but it remains the best introduction. **789** commemorates the tercentenary of the royal charter with the publication of twenty-four lectures. There is an effective 38-page account of the origins and then brief biographies of the founding members. For more controversy about origins, see **42** or articles **X133** and **X420**. **790** is no more and no less than a scholarly study of the Dublin Philosophical Society from 1683 to 1708, examining its membership, aims, organisations and facilities. There is also an appreciation of the contribution the society made to a number of disciplines.

**791.** R. E. W. Maddison, *Life of Robert Boyle* (1968)

**792.** M. S. Fisher, *Robert Boyle, devout naturalist* (1941)

**793.** M. Boas, *Robert Boyle and seventeenth-century chemistry* (1958)

**794.** M. 'Espinasse, *Robert Hooke* (1956)

**791** is a life of Boyle that eschews any attempt to evaluate his scientific achievements and is rather slenderly researched except for his own papers. **792** treats him as a religious conservative, more inclined to compromise his science than his faith when the two were at odds. **793** shows how chemistry achieved respectability as an autonomous discipline during the century – freed from dependence on alchemists and apothecaries – as it developed a programme for understanding the way chemical substances were made out of one another and the way they interacted to make new substances (it is sometimes catalogued under the author's married name, M. B. Hall). **794** is a full-scale, rounded portrait of Boyle's rival, and examines his work as meteorologist, microscopist, instrument-maker and architect.

**795.** F. Manuel, *A portrait of Isaac Newton* (1968)

**796.** A. E. Bell, *Newtonian science* (1961)

**797.** F. Manuel, *The religion of Isaac Newton* (1974)

**798.** B. J. T. Dobbs, *The foundations of Newton's alchemy* (1975)

**799.** T. G. Cowling, *Isaac Newton and astrology* (1977)

**800.** M. C. Jacob, *The Newtonians and the English Revolution, 1689–1720* (1976)

**801.** R. Palmer (ed.), *The annus mirabilis of Sir Isaac Newton* (1968)

**795** is a good, straightforward biography, and is a successful attempt to explain to laymen the revolution in scientific method and practice of which Newton's *Principia* is the great synthesis. **796–9** look at the way Newton remained enthralled by older systems of thought as well as championing new ones, and wrestled to harmonise Mosaic and Newtonian philosophies. **800** examines how churchmen and others took up the new science in the 1690s and beyond and moulded it into their theological system – 'natural religion'. The book argues that such churchmen did more to popularise Newtonianism and to extend its influence than did anyone else. **801** is a collection of sixteen conference papers on general aspects of his life and work. Particularly notable is the contribution by C. Hill on Newton and English society of his time.

**802.** R. S. Porter, *The making of geology* (1977)

This is a lively and wide-ranging discussion of the development of theories of the earth between 1660 and 1815. Only the early part is relevant, but it succeeds in establishing both the intellectual and social context of the development of the subject and is persuasive in showing that seventeenth- and eighteenth-century geologists did not set up a series of obstacles for the nineteenth-century scientists to knock down, but provided the basis – material and conceptual – for later discoveries.

**803.** A. R. Hall, *Ballistics in the seventeenth century* (1952)

**804.** C. Raven, *John Ray, naturalist* (1942)

These two contrasted works both challenge the 'reductionist' view of the subject. **803** relates 'the foundation of the science of ballistics as a mathematical interpretation of some physical problems upon a basis of exact experimental investigation' to the social, economic and scientific background, and concludes that 'in general the conservative tradition of practical men yielded very slowly to the enthusiasm of inventive amateurs'. **804** is intended as a work of theology and shows how Ray's Christianity affected his science more than vice versa. It argues for a Christian view of nature as the 'continually creative manifestation of the creative spirit of God'.

**805.** C. W. Bodemer and L. S. King, *Medical investigation in the seventeenth century* (1968)

**806.** G. Whitteridge, *William Harvey and the circulation of the blood* (1971)

**807.** G. N. Clark, *A history of the Royal College of Physicians of London* (2 vols., 1964)

**805** contains two lectures published together. The first studies the development of embryological thought, particularly in the work of Kenelm Digby (cf. **749**), the second looks at Robert Boyle as a physician (cf. **791–3**). **806** is a detailed study of the intellectual background to Harvey's discovery, and the process by which he came to it. It also considers the reception and defence of his theory in the period 1629–49. **807** is a chronological treatment of its subject, and the last part of volume 1 (1518–1685) and the opening of volume 2 are relevant. It is an institutional history, best chronicling the organisation of the college, its legal status and its struggle against its rivals – the Barber-Surgeons and the Society of Apothecaries. (See also article **X428**.)

# 11
# SCOTLAND, IRELAND and WALES

It would be presumptuous of me to pass judgment in an area where I have no knowledge whatsoever of the source material. It would be easy enough to complain about the lack of work on Irish or Scottish peasants, but there may be overwhelming evidential difficulties. I shall simply content myself with expressing disappointment at the lack of good recent work on Wales (at least in English and at least in comparison with the string of major works which have appeared in recent years on Scottish history). Reading the *Bibliography of Welsh history* (R. T. Jenkins and W. Rees, eds., 1960) and the reviews in *Welsh History Review* since then, I was left puzzled. Could it be that Wales' position was peculiarly disadvantaged by its more thorough integration with England? This both leads to a large number of books appearing with titles concluding '. . . in England and Wales' where the latter principality thereafter gets scant attention, and also means that the market for specifically Welsh books is more restricted. English school children and tertiary students know far more about France, Spain (even the Ottoman Turks) than they do of Wales, and this would remain the case even if half a dozen excellent new books were to appear. Scottish history for our period has been transformed in recent years. Look, for example, at the bibliographies in the standard history of the period (**808**), drawn up in 1964. Only a handful of books are mentioned which had appeared since the second world war. The section on the period of the civil wars, interregnum and reign of Charles II refers to only two books to have appeared since 1924. This chapter lists seven important recent studies and two more – F. Dow on Monck's administration and J. Buckroyd on Lauderdale's – are promised shortly. In contrast, the work on Irish history appears to have unfolded steadily and impressively, with only occasional evidence that the political and confessional strife of that island have spilled over into print. The recent appearance of a major new work of synthesis on the period (**829**) reflects the growing confidence of scholars in its delineation.

## Scotland

**808.** G. Donaldson, *Scotland: James V to James VII* (1965)

**809.** W. Ferguson, *Scotland: 1689 to the present* (1968)

**810.** T. C. Smout, *A history of the Scottish people, 1560–1830* (1969)

These are splendid introductory surveys. The strength of **808** is as a political narrative and in its sure and clear exposition of religious developments. The analytical chapters on the economy, culture and constitutions are a little less probing and clear. For these turn to **810**, which offers little in the way of narrative but builds its treatment of political and religious institutions out of excellent chapters on Scottish economy and society. Both are strongly recommended, **808** for those who like their history 'from above', **810** for those who prefer it 'from below'. **809** is in the same series as **808**, and the early section takes the story through the union. It is noteworthy that Smout sees 1690 rather than 1707 as the great divide, as did Donaldson in planning the series in which his book appears.

**811.** S. G. E. Lythe, *The economy of Scotland in the European setting, 1550–1625* (1960)

A very wide-ranging and important book, which treats its subject topically. It begins by looking at the rural economy, and at food and famine; then at 'enterprise and expansion' (manufactures, fisheries, navigation to Ireland and Nova Scotia); then at governmental action in the control of trade and manufactures and regulation of the currency, credit and prices. But all these are preludes to the major theme which is the diversity and extent of Scotland's trade – with the Baltic, the Netherlands, France, the Mediterranean and England. It concludes that 'under James VI Scotland took a decisive step on the road from one way of life to another'. One regrets the absence of a book of this kind and quality in England. See also **A1** (p. 179).

**812.** W. R. Foster, *The church before the covenants* (1975)

An important study of the successful implementation of a 'hybrid' system of church government in Scotland. It examines (over the period 1560–1637) the institutions of episcopacy, general assemblies, diocesan synods, presbyteries and kirk sessions. Like G. Donaldson and others, the author is complimentary about James VI, and he finds a remarkable commitment to unity and comprehensiveness on all sides.

**813.** D. Mathew, *Scotland under Charles I* (1955)

G. Donaldson's judgment – 'an attempt at a new approach, unsuccessful but containing suggestive ideas' – seems very fair to an outsider. This book attempts to evoke the political and theological aspirations and sensibilities of the opponents of Charles I and also to examine the economic, social and cultural contrasts between regions as a background to the Scots revolt from 1637 onwards.

**814.** D. Stevenson, *The Scottish revolution, 1637–1644* (1973)

**815.** D. Stevenson, *Revolution and counter-revolution in Scotland, 1644–1651* (1977)

These two volumes originally constituted the whole of a vast Ph.D. thesis. They are both marvellously sustained narratives and the author's stated aim is indeed to offer the first account that gets events into order and perspective. Reviewers worried a little about the handling of ecclesiastical complexities and the lack of emphasis on regional contrasts, but agree on the overriding success of the venture. Both books end with an analytical chapter debating the nature of 'the Scottish Revolution': the conclusion in **815** is much the better of the two.

**816.** W. Makey, *The church and the covenant, 1637–1651* (1979)

**817.** F. N. McCoy, *Robert Baillie and the second Scots reformation* (1974)

**818.** L. Kaplan, *Politics and religion during the English Revolution* (1976)

**819.** E. G. Cowan, *For covenant and king* (1977)

**816** is an important complement to **814–15**, since it deals with precisely the area where the above works were weak. The first part offers a chronological account of developments within the covenanting polity, the second part offers a series of analyses of the composition and nature of the covenanting churches and churchmen. **817** is a much less successful work though it too offers a connected narrative of the period 1638–62. Baillie is not important in himself except as a commentator on the events to which he was an intermittent contributor. McCoy places him far too far upstage. But until the appearance of F. Dow's promised book on Monck's government of Scotland (based on an excellent thesis) the chapters on the 1650s are almost the only narrative available (see, however, the relevant chapters in **53** and **169–70**). **818** is one of those annoying books whose title bears little resemblance to the contents. It is in fact an account of the relations between the Scots leaders and the Long Parliament leading up to the signing of the Solemn League and Covenant and the continuing negotiations down to the summer of 1645. Like other books dealing with the internal polities of the Long Parliament it is a confused story, but it provides an additional dimension. Much of it had already appeared in article **X445**. Montrose has had endless weak biographies in the swashbuckling tradition, so that the level-headedness of **819** is a great relief and makes it the new standard narrative, though Scottish reviewers noted factual inaccuracies.

**820.** I. Cowan, *The Scottish covenanters, 1660–1688* (1976)

**821.** W. R. Foster, *Bishop and presbytery: The Church of Scotland, 1661–1688* (1958)

**820** is a brisk, clear and persuasive account of the organisation and tactics of the presbyterians and of the vacillating response of the government. It springs a major surprise by arguing for the success of repression in the 1680s and for the near-extinction of active dissent by 1688. **821** is essentially a study of ecclesiastical administration and of the peaceful coexistence of bishops and presbyterian elements within the Restoration church. It finds that the power and efficacy of the bishops was greater than had been supposed.

**822.** D. Nobbs, *England and Scotland, 1560–1707* (1952)

**823.** G. S. Pryde, *The Treaty of Union of Scotland and England, 1707* (1950)

**824.** T. I. Rae (ed.), *The union of 1707* (1974)

**825.** T. C. Smout, *Scottish trade on the eve of union, 1660–1707* (1963)

**826.** P. W. J. Riley, *The English ministers and Scotland, 1707–1727* (1964)

**822** is a lightweight but balanced account of the debate on the nature of the union of the crowns and/or kingdoms over the period. It is a work of political thought and is lucid as such (it is odd that so little has been done on the aborted Act of Union, 1606–7). **823** is a brief analysis of the passing of the act and a discussion of its consequences. It also includes the full text of the Act and of three attendent acts securing the positions of the churches in each country and of the manner of electing the sixteen representative peers and forty-five commoners to serve in parliament at Westminister. **824** prints six conference papers on the 'impact on Scotland', but some – P. Riley's on the structure of Scottish politics and A. Murray's on administrative arrangements – are of short-term interest and fall within our period. All tend to minimise the impact of the union and argue that it accelerated trends already present. This is also the lesson of **825**, which charts cyclical patterns of stagnation (in times of internal or external war [1640–60, 1689–1715]) and recovery (1580–1640, 1660–90). It is excellent on both the patterns and mechanisms of trade and makes points about smuggling and about the use of Sound Toll Tables which English historians would do well to imitate. **826** is an expanded Ph.D. which examines the administrative problems (particularly with customs and excise) arising from the union. The bulk of the book examines the ministries of Godolphin and Harley. See **A10** (p. 179).

**827.** G. D. Henderson, *Religious life in seventeenth-century Scotland* (1937)

A series of articles on a wide range of subjects: the bible in Scotland; the Scottish pulpit; Scots and the Synod of Dort; Scottish independency; quietism; theological learning, etc.

**828.** A. McKerral, *Kintyre in the seventeenth century* (1948)

This is a brief but thorough account of events in the Kintyre peninsula from 1603 to 1689. It concentrates on the dramatic irruption of national events (e.g. the military progresses of Montrose and David Leslie), on the replacement of the Macdonalds by the Argylls as the dominant family in the region, and on the lowland plantation which had dramatic effects on the culture of the region. There is little on civil or religious government.

## Ireland

**829.** T. W. Moody, F. X. Martin and F. J. Byrne (eds.), *A new history of Ireland*, vol. 3: *1534–1691* (1976)

**830.** J. C. Beckett, *The making of modern Ireland* (1966)

**831.** M. MacCurtain, *Tudor and Stuart Ireland* (1972)

**829** is a quite outstanding survey volume. Built around a series of chronological chapters, but with spacious analytical chapters too on most aspects of Irish history, this is a truly authoritative volume, and must be the starting point for any study of Irish history. It also has an immense bibliography (which is the basis of what follows). **830–1** are interpretative essays. The first 150 pages of **830** offer a cool, crisp survey, best on the social and economic background, perhaps. **831** takes as its theme 'the reduction of the whole country to colonial status'. It too has an allusive brevity and is particularly skilful in its summaries of work on the plantations and the consequent tenurial and agricultural changes.

**832.** R. Bagwell, *Ireland under the Stuarts and during the Interregnum* (3 vols., 1909)

This extended narrative was intended as an equivalent to Gardiner and Firth's volumes on England (**168–70**), and since it uses documents subsequently destroyed in the disastrous fire in Dublin in 1922 which burned most of the Irish public records, it retains some independent value, though now very much superseded by **829**.

**833.** L. M. Cullen, *An economic history of Ireland since 1660* (1973)

**834.** L. M. Cullen, *Anglo-Irish trade, 1660–1800* (1968)

**835.** G. O'Brien, *Economic history of Ireland in the 17th century* (1919)

**836.** E. MacLysaght, *Irish life in the 17th century* (1939, 1950)

Once again, **829** is now the best survey, but all these books are of interest. **833** has two chapters offering a lucid and wide-ranging account of the Irish economy placed in its European setting as well as against the background of discriminating English tariffs and the burdens of war. **834** retains independent interest by focussing more clearly on trade. Cullen argues that Ireland's problems were aggravated but not caused by English policy. **835** is an orderly book divided into four periods: 'construction', 1603–41; 'destruction', 1641–60; 'reconstruction', 1660–89; and 'redestruction' (*sic*), 1689–1700. Each section is then divided into problems of the land, agriculture, mining, manufacturing, trade, finance and coinage. So long as it is used alongside the other books in this section, it is still of value. **836** concentrates on the late seventeenth century. It looks at morals, sports and recreations; at life on the land and in Dublin; at communications; at the clergy, the gentry and their dependents. It is an evocative book with a wealth of illustration. The second edition expands the original by 30,000 words.

**837.** W. A. Phillips (ed.), *A history of the Church of Ireland* (3 vols., 1932–4)

**838.** T. J. Johnston, J. L. Robinson and R. W. Jackson (eds.), *A history of the Church of Ireland* (1953)

**839.** E. R. Bolton, *The Caroline tradition of the Church of Ireland* (1958)

**840.** J. C. Begley, *The Diocese of Limerick in the 16th and 17th century* (1923)

**841.** P. J. Corish (ed.), *A history of Irish Catholicism*, vol. 3 (1968– )

Each volume of **837** consists of a series of separate and substantial essays. The final chapters of volume 2 discuss 'the rise of the Puritans and Planter caste', and the opening part of volume 3 has essays on the reign of Charles I, on the Interregnum (by the author of **839**), on the Restoration and on the Revolution. It is fact-heavy but authoritative in the way textbooks used to be. **838** is a similar format but all in one volume. The seventeenth century thus gets 70 pages, not 350 as in **837**. It is clearly aimed at interested (protestant) laymen. **839** is a curious but intelligent book which finds a distinctive tradition of Irish Anglicanism taking shape in the liturgy, teaching and architecture of Caroline Ireland, which Bolton traces through to the end of the century and beyond. He pays particular attention to Jeremy Taylor (for whom see also **492**). **840** is a long, descriptive work, valuable rather than enervating: diocesan history from above. **841** is appearing piecemeal, with each chapter of each planned volume published as a separate pamphlet. So far only two parts of the sixteenth and seventeenth-century volume have appeared: B. Millett's on 'survival and reorganisation, 1650–1695' and the editor's contribution of which the title, 'the origins of Catholic nationalism', introduces a general account of anti-English resistance throughout the seventeenth century.

**842.** B. Farnell (ed.), *The Irish parliamentary tradition* (1973)

**843.** J. C. Beckett, *Confrontations* (1972)

**842** is a collection of sixteen brief essays which began life as radio talks and which span seven centuries. H. Kearney looks at the early seventeenth century, D. Cregan at the Confederation of Kilkenny, the editor at the Patriot parliament of 1689, and J. G. Simms at the 1690s. **842** is a collection of Becket's published essays, including 'Irish–Scottish relations in the early 17th century' 'The Confederation of Kilkenny reviewed', 'the Irish viceroyalty in the Restoration period' and 'the government of the Church of Ireland under William III and Anne'.

**844.** M. Perceval-Maxwell, *Scottish migration to Ulster in the reign of James I* (1973)

**845.** T. W. Moody, *The Londonderry plantation* (1938)

**846.** K. S. Bottigheimer, *English money and Irish land* (1971)

**844** is a detailed if rather narrowly focussed study of the migrants, where they came from, where they settled and in what numbers – of 'the society that produced the Scottish settlers and of the conditions they encountered when they arrived'. It does not explore motivation so much as context, but it is clear within the limits it sets itself. **845** is a thorough and important study of the bungled Ulster undertaking of the City of London contemporaneous with the Scots settlement. For the clash of interests between city and crown over this venture, see also now **153**. **846** is a computer-aided analysis of the 'adventurers' who speculated in Irish land during the 1640s, of their rewards or otherwise in the 1650s and their fate at the Restoration. It also offers a clear review of parliament's and Cromwell's Irish policies, 1641–58.

**847.** A. Clarke, *The Old English in Ireland, 1625–1642* (1966)

**848.** H. F. Kearney, *Strafford in Ireland, 1633–1641* (1959)

**847** traces the declining influence of the pre-Tudor Norman and English settlers. In practice, the book is a major reappraisal of Irish political and social history in this period. See also the author's kindred articles (**X458–9**). **848** is a major reappraisal of Strafford's government, finding his commercial and land policies less original, and his fiscal and administrative policies more original and successful than had been supposed. See also **X37**, **X460**, **X465**.

**849.** T. C. Barnard, *Cromwellian Ireland* (1975)

**850.** St J. D. Seymour, *The puritans in Ireland* (1912, 1969)

**851.** P. B. Ellis, *To Hell or Connaught!* (1971)

**852.** D. Esson, *The curse of Cromwell* (1971)

**849** is a major reassessment of the aims and achievements of the Interregnum regimes in Ireland. It analyses their policies towards finance, trade, religion, education, the 'advancement of learning' and the law. It emphasises how influential groups in England saw Ireland as the test-bed for schemes they hoped to implement at home, and also how from the mid-1650s on, practical considerations led to a tempering of the earlier severe anti-Catholic policies (the latter is summarised in article **X453**). It almost completely supersedes **850**, which however retains some value for its narrative, particularly of the later 1640s. The author claims to 'have written from the standpoint of a clergyman of the Church of Ireland but to have treated the other protestant denominations of the period with scrupulous fairness'. One is, nonetheless, suprised to find no mention of the Catholic majority in the index or much elsewhere! **851–2** are popular works written from the most available sources, the first describing the course of the Connaught plantation, the second Cromwell's conquest of Ireland (1649–53) and settlement policy.

**853.** K. M. Lynch, *Roger Boyle, first earl of Orrery* (1965)

A straightforward biography, quite fully researched, of the man known to Interregnum scholars as Lord Broghil, conservative ally of Cromwell, and to Restoration scholars as the earl of Orrery, lord president of Munster.

**854.** J. G. Simms, *Jacobite Ireland, 1685–1691* (1969)

**855.** P. B. Ellis, *The Boyne water* (1976)

**856.** C. D. Milligan, *History of the siege of Londonderry, 1689* (1952)

**854** is a full political and military history of Ireland in these years in narrative form. It is thoroughly researched and dispassionate. **855** is a straightforward, derivative narrative of the campaign of 1690, while **856** is a full but triumphalist account of 'the courage and determination of the British people (which) reaches its greatest heights in the defence of its liberties against the forces of oppression'.

**857.** J. G. Simms, *The Williamite confiscation in Ireland, 1690–1703* (1956)

**858.** J. C. Beckett, *Protestant dissent in Ireland, 1687–1780* (1947)

**857** shows that the expropriation of the Catholic landowners in the 1690s, though extensive (their share fell by a third) was not as extensive as was previously supposed. It also examines the political and constitutional issues raised by the forfeitures. **858** is a study of the imposition of a sacramental test after the revolution and at dissenting protestant reaction. A chronological account is followed by an analysis of four aspects of persecution.

## Wales

**859.** D. Williams, *A history of modern Wales* (1950)

**860.** H. Thomas, *A history of Wales, 1485–1660* (1971)

**861.** E. D. Evans, *A history of Wales, 1660–1815* (1976)

It cannot be denied that these textbooks do not have the weight or the depth of the main Irish and Scottish textbooks (**808–9**, **829–31**). **859** is a brisk, purposeful history devoting eighty pages to the seventeenth century, stressing religious developments. **860–1** are designed as student textbooks and offer wide-ranging summaries not only of political and religious but of educational, cultural, social and economic developments. One only regrets the lack of a chapter on local government and law-and-order.

**862.** A. H. Dodd, *Studies in Stuart Wales* (1952)

A series of related essays which sets out to disprove the tendency of others 'to regard the history of Wales in the 17th century as a comparatively insignificant interpolation between the age of the Tudors and the stirring times of the Methodist Revival'. The essays look at the social order, at Ludlow's role as a capital of early Stuart Wales, at the political, economic and cultural links between Ireland and Wales, at the government of Wales during the mid-century troubles, and at the rise of party at the end of the century.

**863.** G. Williams (ed.), *Glamorgan County History*, vol. 4: *1536–c. 1770* (1974)

**864.** A. H. Dodd, *History of Caernarvonshire* (1968)

863 is an excellent series of essays, roughly akin to the *Victoria County Histories* for English counties. There are four chapters on different aspects of the period 1536–1642, two covering 1642–60, and four more topics in the period 1660–1770. Subjects include the economy, society, religion, politics and administration, and education. The editor leads from the front with three outstanding contributions, above all in his account of social structure and social

mobility. **864** is a model compact county history with about a hundred pages on the seventeenth century. It is basically a political narrative but economic, social and religious developments are subsumed into the text. But for local government see now **X474**.

**865.** H. A. Lloyd, *The gentry of south-west Wales, 1540–1640* (1978)

An important study of the poor, backward, insular gentry of Carmarthenshire, Cardigan and Pembrokeshire with looks at their estates, incomes, formal and informal power, religion and culture. It finds them possessing 'a self-centred apathy to external affairs'.

**866.** N. Tucker, *North Wales in the civil war* (n.d., but 1958?)

**867.** A. L. Lynch, *Pembrokeshire in the civil war* (1937)

**866** is a congested and sometimes confusing account of the first and second civil war, based on the most obvious primary and secondary sources, but no more. **867** is again fairly lightly researched, but is much more perceptive and balanced. See also **A8** (p. 179).

**868.** T. Richards, *History of the puritan movement in Wales, 1639–1653* (1920)

**869.** T. Richards, *Religious developments in Wales, 1654–1662* (1923)

**870.** T. Richards, *Wales under the penal code, 1662–1687* (1923)

**871.** T. Richards, *Wales under the indulgence, 1672–1675* (1928)

Four infuriating works which present a vast, disorganised body of material in a peculiarly unhelpful fashion. It can only be described as ill-digested antiquarianism. Yet on most issues they remain the only works available.

**872.** G. Nuttall, *The Welsh saints* (1957)

Studies of Walter Craddock (an antinomian), Vavasor Powell (Fifth Monarchist) and Morgan Lloyd (mystic) which find a common denominator in the sponsorship of all three in the puritan circle around the Harleys of Brampton Bryan. It is mainly a work of theology, but is of wide interest. I am assured that there is a splendid biography of Vavasor Powell by R. T. Jones, but it is in Welsh.

**873.** G. H. Jenkins, *Literature, religion and society in Wales, 1660–1730* (1978)

This book challenges the view that between the early Reformation and the coming of Methodism Welsh religion went through a torpid and dull period. By analysing the widespread distribution and use of Welsh bibles, prayer books and catechisms, by considering the work of 140 authors, and by looking at printing in Welsh and at the book trade, Jenkins is able to offer a major re-evaluation of the cultural life of Wales, and a corrective to the over-simplified accounts which see Methodism as growing out of a response to Anglican abuses or out of a phoenix-like recrudescence of nationalism.

# APPENDIX: ARTICLE LITERATURE (1958–79)

The problems of selection in this section are more acute. Well over a hundred relevant articles appear every year, and the quality varies enormously. The task of reading and judging them all is too daunting for one hard-pressed academic! Instead I have decided to gather together what is intended as a group of important articles published since 1957. They may well not be the only important articles, but they should cover most of the ground. The year 1957 was chosen because that is the year Mrs Keeler stopped her search for articles when she was editing the standard bibliography of the period (see **1**). This appendix is thus a partial supplement to her work. My other major restriction was to concentrate on what I take to be the twenty-seven most important periodicals which regularly publish articles on seventeenth-century British history. I made a search of all copies of those periodicals published between 1 January 1958 and 1 September 1979 and browsed every item that seemed to be of interest. Most but not all relevant items have been included. I then added to that list such articles from other periodicals as I already knew and already recommended to my pupils from time to time. The result may be an unhappy compromise, and I would not defend it on any but empirical grounds as a working compilation of some of the best work available. I was amazed how many articles on subjects I am interested in had never come my way before, and I hope most users of this book will feel likewise. The periodicals scoured were:

| | (abbreviation) |
|---|---|
| *Agricultural History Review* | *AgHR* |
| *American Historical Review* | *AmHR* |
| *Britain and the Netherlands* | *B & N* |
| *Bulletin of the Institute of Historical Research* | *BIHR* |
| *Church History* | *ChH* |
| *Economic History Review* (2nd series) | *EcHR* |
| *English Historical Review* | *EHR* |
| *Historical Association Pamphlets* (general series) | *HAP* |
| *Historical Journal* | *HJ* |
| *History* | *H* |
| *History of Science* | *HSc* |
| *History and Theory* | *HTh* |
| *Irish Historical Studies* | *IHS* |
| *Journal of British Studies* | *JBS* |
| *Journal of Ecclesiastical History* | *JEccH* |
| *Journal of the History of Ideas* | *JHI* |
| *Journal of Modern History* | *JMH* |
| *Journal of Religious History* | *JRH* |

| | |
|---|---|
| *Midland History* | *MH* |
| *Northern History* | *NH* |
| *Past and Present* | *PP* |
| *Scottish Historical Review* | *ScHR* |
| *Social History* | *SH* |
| *Studies in Church History* | *SCH* |
| *Transactions of the Royal Historical Society* (5th series) | *TRHS* |
| *University of Birmingham Historical Journal* | *UBHJ* |
| *Welsh History Review* | *WHR* |

Two of these are not straightforward historical periodicals: *Britain and the Netherlands* are the proceedings of the triennial Anglo-Dutch Historical Conferences and contain some key articles which deserve wider circulation. Volumes 1–5 are edited by [and often catalogued by libraries under] J. S. Bromley and E. Kossman, vol. 6 by A. Duke and C. Tamse; while *Studies in Church History* are the transactions of the (now) annual ecclesiastical conference. There are sixteen volumes to date. Each volume from volume 4 has its own theme. Volume 1 was edited by C. W. Dugmore and C. Duggan, vols. 2–8 by G. J. Cuming, and vol. 9 onwards by D. Baker. The appendix also contains articles from the following:

| | (abbreviation) |
|---|---|
| *Albion* | *Albion* |
| *American Journal of Legal History* | *AJLH* |
| *Business History* | *Bus. Hist.* |
| *Daedalus* | *Daedalus* |
| *Guildhall Miscellany* | *Guildhall Misc.* |
| *Historical Studies* (Ireland) | *HS* |
| *Historical Studies* (Australia and New Zealand) | *HS(A&NZ)* |
| *History Today* | *HT* |
| *Huntington Library Quarterly* | *HLQ* |
| *Journal of Economic History* | *JEconH* |
| *Journal of European Economic History* | *JEurEcH* |
| *Journal of Interdisciplinary History* | *JIDH* |
| *Journal of Peasant Studies* | *JPS* |
| *Journal of the Society of Archivists* | *JSA* |
| *Literature and History* | *Lit&Hist* |
| *Local Population Studies* | *LPS* |
| *London Journal* | *Lond.J.* |
| *Medical History* | *Med.Hist* |
| *Recusant History* | *Rec.Hist.* |
| *Scandinavian Economic History Review* | *ScEcHR* |
| *War and Society* | *W&S* |

### Government
(see chapter 2)

**X1.** G. E. Aylmer, Charles I's Commission on Fees, *BIHR* 31 (1958)

**X2.** G. E. Aylmer, Office holding as a factor in English history, 1625–1642, *H* 44 (1959)

**X3.** G. E. Aylmer, The last years of Purveyance, 1610–1660, *EcHR* 12 (1959–60)

**X4.** T. G. Barnes, Star Chamber mythology, *AJLH* 5 (1961)

**X5.** T. G. Barnes, Due process and slow process in Elizabethan and early Stuart Star Chamber, *AJLH* 6 (1962)

**X6.** J. V. Beckett, Local custom and the 'new taxation' in the 17th and 18th centuries, *NH* 12 (1976)

**X7.** C. Brooks, Public finance and political stability: the administration of the land tax, 1688–1720, *HJ* 17 (1974)

**X8.** J. V. Jensen, The staff of the Jacobean Privy Council, *HLQ* 40 (1976)

**X9.** D. R. Kelley, History, English law and the Renaissance, *PP* 65 (1974)

**X10.** C. J. Kitching, Probate during the civil war and interregnum, *JSA* 5 (1976)

**X11.** M. Lee, The Jacobean diplomatic device, *AmHR* 72 (1966)

**X12.** J. C. Sainty, A reform in the tenure of offices during the reign of Charles II, *BIHR* 41 (1968)

**X13.** B. Shapiro, Law reform in seventeenth-century England, *AJLH* 19 (1975)

**X14.** G. W. Thomas, James I, Equity and Lord Keeper Williams, *EHR* 91 (1976)

**X15.** H. C. Tomlinson, Place and Profit: an examination of the Ordnance Office, 1660–1714, *TRHS* 25 (1975)

**X16.** H. C. Tomlinson, The Ordnance Office and the navy, 1660–1714, *EHR* 90 (1975)

### Political history
(see chapter 3)

**X17.** D. Allen, The role of the London trained bands in the Exclusion Crisis, *EHR* 87 (1972)

**X18.** D. Allen, Political clubs in Restoration London, *HJ* 19 (1976)

**X19.** J. Alsop, Gerrard Winstanley's later life, *PP* 82 (1979)

**X20.** C. B. Anderson, Ministerial responsibility in the 1620s, *JMH* 34 (1962)

**X21.** S. D. Antler, Quantitative analysis of the Long Parliament, *PP* 56 (1972) [debate 58]

**X22.** N. P. Bard, The Ship Money case and William Fiennes, Viscount Saye and Sele, *BIHR* 50 (1977)

**X23.** T. G. Barnes, County politics and a Puritan cause célèbre: Somerset Churchales, 1633, *TRHS* 9 (1959)

**X24.** R. Beddard, The Guildhall Declaration of 11 December 1688 and the counter-revolution of the loyalists, *HJ* 11 (1968)

**X25.** G. V. Bennett, Robert Harley, the Godolphin Ministry and the Bishoprics crisis of 1707, *EHR* 82 (1967)

**X26.** L. Boynton, Billeting: the example of the Isle of Wight, *EHR* 74 (1959)

**X27.** L. Boynton, Martial law and the Petition of Right, *EHR* 79 (1964)

**X28.** R. Brenner, The civil war politics of London's merchant community, *PP* 58 (1973)

**X29.** D. E. Brewster and R. Howell, Reconsidering the Levellers: The evidence of *The Moderate*, *PP* 46 (1970)

**X30.** A. Carpenter, William King and the threats to the Church of Ireland during the reign of James II, *IHS* 18 (1972–3)

**X31.** J. Carter, Cabinet records for the reign of William III, *EHR* 78 (1963)

**X32.** G. L. Cherry, The Role of the Convention Parliament (1688–9) in parliamentary sovereignty, *JHI* 17 (1958)

**X33.** P. Christianson, The causes of the English Revolution: a reappraisal, *JBS* 15 (1975)

**X34.** P. Christianson, The peers, the people and parliamentary management in the first six months of the Long Parliament, *JMH* 49 (1977)

**X35.** P. Clark, Thomas Scott and the growth of urban opposition to the early Stuarts, *HJ* 21 (1978)

**X36.** R. Clifton, The popular fear of Catholics during the English Revolution, *PP* 52 (1971)

**X37.** J. P. Cooper, The fortune of Thomas Wentworth, earl of Strafford, *EcHR* 11 (1958–9)

**X38.** E. S. Cope, The short Parliament of 1640 and Convocation, *JEccH* 25 (1974)

**X39.** E. S. Cope, John Rushworth and the Short Parliament of 1640, *BIHR* 51 (1978)

**X40.** M. Cotterell, Interregnum law reform: the Hale Commission of 1652, *EHR* 83 (1968)

**X41.** A. N. B. Cotton, Cromwell and the Self-Denying Ordinance, *H* 61 (1977)

**X42.** P. Crawford, "Charles Stuart, that man of blood", *JBS* 16 (1977)

**X43.** P. Croft, Free trade and the House of Commons, 1605–6, *EcHR* 28 (1975)

**X44.** E. Cruickshanks, The Tories and the succession to the throne in the 1714 Parliament, *BIHR* 46 (1973)

**X45.** M. H. Curtis, The alienated intellectuals of early Stuart England, *PP* 23 (1962) [see **41**]

**X46.** J. C. Davis, The Levellers and democracy, *PP* 40 (1968) [see **183, 314, X29**]

**X47.** J. C. Davis, Gerrard Winstanley and the restoration of true magistracy, *PP* 70 (1976)

**X48.** B. Donagan, Greed and consistency in the life of the earl of Holland, *HJ* 19 (1976)

**X49.** J. A. Downie, The Commission of Public Accounts and the formation of the country party, *EHR* 91 (1976)

**X50.** C. A. Edie, New buildings, new taxes and old interests: an urban problem of the 1670s, *JBS* 6 (1967)

**X51.** C. A. Edie, Charles II, the Commons, and the Newark Charter dispute, *JBS* 10 (1970)

**X52.** C. A. Edie, The popular idea of monarchy on the eve of the Stuart Restoration, *HLQ* 39 (1976)

**X53.** K. S. van Eerde, The Jacobean baronets: an issue between king and parliament, *JMH* 33 (1961)

**X54.** J. Engberg, Royalist finances in the English civil war, *ScEcHR* 16 (1968)

**X55.** H. R. Engstrom, Sir Arthur Haselrige: the forgotten knight of the Long Parliament, *Albion* 8 (1976)

**X56.** J. E. Farnell, The usurpation of honest London householders: Barebone's Parliament, *EHR* 82 (1967)

**X57.** J. E. Farnell, The aristocracy and leadership of parliament on the English civil wars, *JMH* 44 (1972)

**X58.** J. E. Farnell, The social and intellectual basis of London's role in the English civil wars, *JMH* 49 (1977)

**X59.** J. S. Flemion, The struggle for the Petition of Right in the House of Lords: the study of an opposition party victory, *JMH* 45 (1973)

**X60.** J. S. Flemion, Slow process, due process and the High Court of Parliament: a reinterpretation of the revival of judicature in the House of Lords in 1621, *HJ* 17 (1974)

**X61.** J. S. Flemion, The nature of opposition in the House of Lords in the early seventeenth century, *Albion* 8 (1976)

**X62.** E. R. Foster, Procedure in the House of Lords during the early Stuart period, *JBS* 5 (1966)

**X63.** E. R. Foster, Petitions and Petitions of Right, *JBS* 14 (1974)

**X64.** E. R. Foster, The House of Lords and Ordinances, 1641–9, *AJLH* 21 (1977)

**X65.** S. Foster, The Presbyterian-Independents exorcised: a ghost story for historians, *PP* 44 (1969) [debate 47]

**X66.** I. Gentles, Arrears of pay and ideology in the army revolt of 1647, *W&S* 1 (1977)

**X67.** I. Gentles, London Levellers in the English Revolution: the Chidleys and their circle, *JEccH* 29 (1978)

**X68.** L. Glow, Pym and Parliament: the methods of moderation, *JMH* 36 (1964)

**X69.** L. Glow, Political affiliations in the House of Commons after Pym's death, *BIHR* 38 (1965)

**X70.** L. Glow, The Committee of Safety (1642–3), *EHR* 80 (1965)

**X71.** L. Glow, The manipulation of committees in the Long Parliament, 1640–1642, *JBS* 5 (1965)

**X72.** E. Gregg, Was Queen Anne a Jacobite?, *H* 57 (1972)

**X73.** E. Gregg, Marlborough in exile, 1712–14, *HJ* 15 (1972)

**X74.** J. K. Gruenfelder, The electoral patronage of Sir Thomas Wentworth, earl of Strafford, 1614–1640, *JMH* 49 (1977)

**X75.** K. D. H. Haley, Charles II, *HAP* G63

**X76.** K. D. H. Haley, 'No popery' in the reign of Charles II, *B&N* 5 (1975)

**X77.** G. Hammersley, The revival of the forest laws under Charles I, *H* 45 (1960)

**X78.** A. Hast, State treason trials during the Puritan Revolution, *HJ* 15 (1972)

**X79.** G. D. Heath, The making of the Instrument of Government, *JBS* 6 (1967)

**X80.** J. H. Hexter, The English aristocracy, its crises and the English Revolution, 1558–1660, *JBS* 7 (1967)

**X81.** J. H. Hexter, Power struggle, parliament and liberty in early Stuart England, *JMH* 50 (1978)

**X82.** B. W. Hill, Oxford, Bolingbroke and the Peace of Utrecht, *HJ* 16 (1973)

**X83.** C. Hill, Oliver Cromwell, *HAP* G 38

**X84.** R. W. K. Hinton, The decline of parliamentary government under Elizabeth I and the early Stuarts, *CHJ* 13 (1957)

**X85.** D. Hirst, The defection of Sir Edward Dering 1640–41, *HJ* 15 (1972)

**X86.** D. Hirst, Elections and privileges in the House of Commons in the early 17th century, *HJ* 18 (1975)

**X87.** D. Hirst, Unanimity in the Commons, aristocratic intrigue, and the origins of the English civil war, *JMH* 50 (1978)

**X88.** D. Hirst, The Privy Council and problems of enforcement in the 1620s, *JBS* 18 (1978)

**X89.** C. Holmes, Colonel King and Lincolnshire politics 1642–46, *HJ* 16 (1973)

**X90.** G. S. Holmes, Religion and politics in late Stuart England, *HAP* G 86

**X91.** G. S. Holmes, The Sacheverell Riots: the crowd and the church in early 18th century London, *PP* 72 (1976)

**X92.** G. S. Holmes and W. Speck, The fall of Harley in 1708, *EHR* 80 (1965)

**X93.** H. Horwitz, Parties, connections and parliamentary politics, 1689–1714, *JBS* 6 (1966)

**X94.** H. Horwitz, The general election of 1690, *JBS* 11 (1971)

**X95.** H. Horwitz, Parliament and the Glorious Revolution *BIHR* 47 (1974)

**X96.** D. H. Hosford, Bishop Compton and the revolution of 1688, *JEccH* 23 (1972)

**X97.** G. F. T. Jones, The composition and leadership of the Presbyterian party in the Convention, *EHR* 79 (1960)

**X98.** G. F. T. Jones, The Bristol affair, 1663, *JRH* 5 (1968–9)

**X99.** G. H. Jones, The problem of French protestantism in the foreign policy of England, 1680–8, *BIHR* 42 (1969)

**X100.** J. R. Jones, James II's Whig collaborators, *HJ* 3 (1960)

**X101.** J. R. Jones, Political groups and tactics in the Convention of 1660, *HJ* 6 (1963)

**X102.** J. R. Jones, English attitudes to Europe in the 17th century, *B&N* 3 (1968)

**X103.** L. Kaplan, Presbyterians and Independents in 1643, *EHR* 84 (1969)

**X104.** L. Kaplan, The 'plot' to depose Charles I in 1644, *BIHR* 44 (1971)

**X105.** D. E. Kennedy, The English naval revolt of 1648, *EHR* 77 (1962)

**X106.** R. W. Kenny, The parliamentary influence of Charles Howard, earl of Nottingham, 1536–1624, *JMH* 39 (1967)

**X107.** M. Kishlansky, The sales of crown lands and the spirit of the revolution, *EcHR* 29 (1976)

**X108.** M. Kishlansky, The emergence of adversary politics in the Long Parliament, *JMH* 49 (1977)

**X109.** M. Kishlansky, The case of the army truly stated: the creation of the New Model Army, *PP* 81 (1978)

**X110.** P. S. Lachs, Advice and consent: parliament and foreign policy under the late Stuarts, *Albion* 7 (1975)

**X111.** K. J. Lindley, The impact of the 1641 rebellion on England and Wales, *IHS* 18 (1972–3)

**X112.** Tai Liu, The calling of Barebone's Parliament reconsidered, *JEccH* 22 (1971)

**X113.** J. I. McGuire, Why was Ormonde dismissed in 1669? *IHS* 18 (1972

**X114.** J. J. N. McGurk, The clergy and the militia, 1580–1610, *H* 60 (1975)

**X115.** J. J. N. McGurk, Royal purveyance in the Shire of Kent, 1590–1614, *BIHR* 50 (1977)

**X116.** A. MacInnes, The political ideas of Robert Harley, *H* 50 (1965)

**X117.** M. Mahony, Presbyterianism and the City of London, 1645–7, *HJ* 22 (1979)

**X118.** J. L. Malcolm, A king in search of soldiers: Charles I in 1642, *HJ* 21 (1978)

**X119.** B. S. Manning, The peasantry and the English Revolution, *JPS* 2 (1975)

**X120.** J. G. Marston, Gentry honor and royalism in early Stuart England, *JBS* 13 (1973)

**X121.** C. R. Mayes, The sale of peerages in early Stuart England, *JMH* 29 (1957)

**X122.** C. R. Mayes, The early Stuarts and the Irish peerage, *EHR* 73 (1958)

**X123.** J. Miller, Catholic officers in the later Stuart army, *EHR* 88 (1973)

**X124.** J. Miller, The militia and the army in the reign of James II, *HJ* 16 (1973)

**X125.** J. Miller, The correspondence of Edward Coleman, 1674–8, *Rec. Hist.* 14 (1978)

**X126.** T. K. Moore and H. Horwitz, Who runs the House? Aspects of parliamentary organization in the later 17th century, *JMH* 43 (1971)

**X127.** J. S. Morrill, Mutiny and discontent in English provincial armies, *PP* 56 (1972)

**X128.** J. S. Morrill, The army revolt of 1647, *B&N* 6 (1978)

**X129.** J. S. Morrill, The northern gentry and the Great Rebellion, *NH* 15 (1979)

**X130.** L. Mulligan, The Committee Men in the Long Parliament, *HJ* 8 (1965)

**X131.** L. Mulligan *et alii*, Winstanley: a case for the man as he said he was, *JEccH* 28 (1967)

**X132.** L. Mulligan, Peace negotiations, politics and the Committee of Both Kingdoms, *HJ* 12 (1969)

**X133.** L. Mulligan, Civil war politics, religion and the Royal Society, *PP* 59 (1973)

**X134.** L. Mulligan, Property and parliamentary politics in the English civil war, 1642–1646, *HS(A&NZ)* 16 (1975)

**X135.** R. C. Munden, The defeat of Sir John Fortescue: court versus country at the Hustings, *EHR* 93 (1978)

**X136.** P. R. Newman, Catholic royalist activists in the North, 1642–46, *Rec. Hist.* 14 (1977)

**X137.** G. B. Nourse, Richard Cromwell's House of Commons, *BJRL* 60 (1977)

**X138.** V. Pearl, Oliver St John and the 'middle group' in the Long Parliament, *EHR* 81 (1966)

**X139.** V. Pearl, The 'Royal Independents' in the English civil war, *TRHS* 18 (1968)

**X140.** L. L. Peck, Problems in Jacobean administration: was Henry Howard, earl of Northampton, a reformer? *HJ* 19 (1976)

**X141.** D. H. Pennington, The

cost of the English civil war, *HT* 8 (1958)

**X142.** P. J. Pinckney, Scottish representation in the Cromwellian parliament of 1656, *ScHR* 46 (1967)

**X143.** J. H. Plumb, The growth of the electorate in England from 1600 to 1715, *PP* 45 (1969)

**X144.** T. K. Rabb, Sir Edwin Sandys and the Parliament of 1604, *AmHR* 69 (1963)

**X145.** P. W. J. Riley, The union of 1707 as an episode in English politics, *EHR* 84 (1969)

**X146.** C. Roberts, The constitutional significance of the financial settlement of 1690, *HJ* 20 (1977)

**X147.** C. Roberts, The earl of Bedford and the coming of the English Revolution, *JMH* 49 (1977)

**X148.** C. Roberts and O. Duncan, The Parliamentary Undertaking of 1614, *EHR* 93 (1978)

**X149.** M. Roberts, Cromwell and the Baltic, *EHR* 76 (1961)

**X150.** I. Roy, The royalist Council of War, 1642–6, *BIHR* 35 (1962)

**X151.** I Roy, The English civil war and English society, *W&S* 1 (1977)

**X152.** I. Roy, England turned Germany? the aftermath of the civil war in its European context, *TRNS* 28 (1978)

**X153.** D. Rubini, Politics and the battle for the banks, 1688–1697, *EHR* 85 (1970)

**X154.** H. Rusche, Astrology and propaganda, 1644–1651, *EHR* 80 (1965)

**X155.** H. Rusche, Prophecies and propaganda, 1641–1651, *EHR* 84 (1969)

**X156.** C. Russell, The Ship Money judgments of Bramston and Davenport, *EHR* 77 (1962)

**X157.** C. Russell, The theory of treason in the trial of Strafford, *EHR* 80 (1965)

**X158.** C. Russell, Parliamentary history in perspective, 1604–1628, *H* 61 (1976)

**X159.** C. Russell, The foreign policy debate in the House of Commons in 1621, *HJ* 20 (1977)

**X160.** W. L. Sachse, The mob in the Revolution of 1688, *JBS* 4 (1964)

**X161.** W. L. Sachse, An analysis of the Regicide Court, *JBS* 12 (1973)

**X162.** M. L. Schwartz, James I and the historians, *JBS* 13 (1974)

**X163.** L. G. Schwoerer, 'The fittest subject for a king's quarrel: an essay on the militia controversy, 1641–1642, *JBS* 11 (1971)

**X164.** L. G. Schwoerer, Press and Parliament in the Revolution of 1689, *HJ* 20 (1977)

**X165.** L. G. Schwoerer, Propaganda in the Revolution of 1688–9, *AmHR* 82 (1977)

**X166.** R. M. Smuts, The puritan followers of Henrietta-Maria in the 1630s, *EHR* 93 (1978)

**X167.** V. F. Snow, Parliamentary reapportionment proposals in the Puritan Revolution, *EHR* 74 (1959)

**X168.** V. F. Snow, Essex and the aristocratic opposition to the early Stuarts, *JMH* 32 (1960)

**X169.** W. A. Speck, The choice of a Speaker in 1705, *BIHR* 37 (1964)

**X170.** R. T. Spence, The pacification of the Cumberland borders, 1593–1628, *NH* 13 (1977)

**X171.** S. J. Stearns, Conscription and English society in the 1620s, *JBS* 11 (1972)

**X172.** R. A. Stradling, Spanish conspiracy in England, 1661–3, *EHR* 87 (1972)

**X173.** R. J. W. Swales, The Ship Money levy of 1628, *BIHR* 50 (1977)

**X174.** B. Taft, The Humble Petition of Several Colonels of the Army, *HLQ* 42 (1979)

**X175.** K. Thomas, Women and the civil war sects, *PP* 13 (1958) [see **41**]

**X176.** C. Thompson, The origins of the politics of the Parliamentary middle group, *TRHS* 22 (1972)

**X177.** M. A. Thomson, Louis XIV and William III, *EHR* 76 (1961) [see **282**]

**X178.** P. Torntoft, William III and Denmark–Norway, 1697–1702, *EHR* 81 (1966)

**X179.** D. Underdown, Party management in the recruiter elections, 1645–1648, *EHR* 83 (1968)

**X180.** D. Underdown, Cromwell and the officers, February 1658, *EHR* 83 (1968)

**X181.** C. V. Wedgwood *et al.*, Charles I, *HAP* G11

**X182.** A. Woolrych, Penruddock's Rising, 1655, *HAP* G 29

**X183.** A. Woolrych, The calling of Barebone's Parliament, *EHR* 80 (1965)

**X184.** M. B. Young, Illusions of grandeur and reform at the Jacobean court: Cranfield and the Ordnance, *HJ* 22 (1979)

### Political and constitutional thought (see chapter 4)

**X185.** J. Appleby, Ideology and theory: the tension between political and economic liberalism in 17th century England, *AmHR* 81 (1976)

**X186.** W. F. Bynum, The Great Chain of Being after forty years, *HSc* 13 (1975)

**X187.** J. P. Cooper, Differences between English and continental governments in the early 17th century, *B&N* 1 (1960)

**X188.** J. W. Daly, Could Charles I be trusted? The royalist case, 1642–1646, *JBS* 6 (1966)

**X189.** J. W. Daly, John Bramhall and the theoretical problems of royalist moderation, *JBS* 11 (1971)

**X190.** J. Daly, The idea of absolute monarchy in 17th century England, *HJ* 21 (1978)

**X191.** G. Drake, The ideology of Oliver Cromwell, *ChH* 35 (1966)

**X192.** J. Dunn, Consent in the political theory of John Locke, *HJ* 10 (1967)

**X193.** C. A. Edie, Succession and monarchy: the controversy of 1679–1681, *AmHR* 70 (1964)

**X194.** M. J. Enright, King James and his island: an archaic kingship belief? *ScHR* 55 (1976)

**X195.** M. Goldie, Edmund Bohun and the *Ius Gentium* in the Revolution debate, 1689–1693, *HJ* 20 (1977)

**X196.** J. W. Gough, James Tyrrell: Whig historian and friend of John Locke, *HJ* 19 (1976)

**X197.** W. H. Greenleaf, James I and the Divine Right of Kings, *HT* 14 (1964)

**X198.** J. A. W. Gunn, The *Civil Polity* of Peter Paxton, *PP* 40 (1968) [see **312**]

**X199.** R. W. K. Hinton, English constitutional theories from Sir John Fortescue to Sir John Eliot, *EHR* 75 (1960)

**X200.** R. MacGillivray, A study of Hobbes' *Behemoth, JHI* 31 (1970)

**X201.** J. C. Morrison, Philosophy and history in Bacon, *JHI* 38 (1977)

**X202.** F. Oakley, The political thought of John Mayor and George Buchanan, *JBS* 1 (1962)

**X203.** K. Olivecrona, Locke on origin of property, *JHI* 35 (1974)

**X204.** R. R. Orr, Chillingworth versus Hooker: A criticism of natural law theory, *JRH* 2 (1962–3)

**X205.** J. G. A. Pocock, James Harrington and the Good Old Cause, *JBS* 9 (1969)

**X206.** J. Sanderson, The royalism of John Bramhall, *JEccH* 25 (1974)

**X207.** J. Schochet, Patriarchalism, politics and mass attitudes in Stuart England, *HJ* 12 (1969)

**X208.** Q. Skinner, History and ideology in the English Revolution, *HJ* 8 (1965)

**X209.** Q. Skinner, The ideological context of Hobbes' political thought, *HJ* 9 (1966)

**X210.** V. F. Snow, The concept of revolution in 17th century England, *HJ* 5 (1962)

**X211.** G. Straka, The final phase of divine right theory in England, 1688–1702, *EHR* 77 (1962)

**X212.** C. D. Tarlton, Interpreting Locke's Firts Treatise of Government, *HJ* 21 (1978)

**X213.** M. P. Thompson, The

idea of conquest: 1688 Revolution, *JHI* 38 (1977)

**X214.** M. Walzer, Puritanism as a revolutionary ideology, *HTh* 3 (1964)

**X215.** D. H. J. Warner, Hobbes' interpretation of the Doctrine of the Trinity, *JRH* 5 (1968–9)

**X216.** C. C. Weston, The theory of mixed monarchy under Charles I and after, *EHR* 75 (1960)

**X217.** R. Willman, The origins of 'Whig' and 'Tory' in English political language, *HJ* 17 (1974)

**X218.** P. Zagorin, The court and country: a note on political terminology in the earlier 17th century, *EHR* 77 (1962)

**Ecclesiastical history (see chapter 6)**

**X219.** J. C. H. Aveling, The marriages of Catholic recusants, 1559–1642, *JEccH* 14 (1963)

**X220.** C. Bangs, The enigma of Arminian politics, *ChH* 42 (1973)

**X221.** R. A. Beddard, The Commission for Ecclesiastical Promotions, 1681–84, *HJ* 10 (1967)

**X222.** R. A. Beddard, Vincent Alsop and the emancipation of Restoration dissenters, *JEccH* 24 (1973)

**X223.** G. V. Bennett, The convocation of 1710, *SCH* 7 (1970)

**X224.** G. V. Bennett, The Seven Bishops – a reconsideration, *SCH* 15 (1978)

**X225.** H. T. Blethen, The altar controversy and the royal supremacy, 1627–1641, *WHR* 9 (1978)

**X226.** M. F. Brass, Reduction of episcopacy as a means of unity in England, 1640–1662, *ChH* 30 (1962)

**X227.** I. Breward, The abolition of puritanism, *JRH* 7 (1972–3)

**X228.** T. L. Canavan, Burton, Swift and anti-Puritan invective, *JHI* 34 (1973)

**X229.** P. Collinson, Lectures by combination: structures and characteristics of church life in 17th century England, *BIHR* 48 (1975)

**X230.** S. G. Cook, The Congregational Independents and the Cromwellian constitutions, *ChH* 46 (1977)

**X231.** M. C. Cross, Achieving the millennium – the church in York during the commonwealth, *SCH* 4 (1967)

**X232.** M. C. Cross, Protestant protest against Catholic foundations, 1540–1640, *SCH* 9 (1972)

**X233.** G. J. Cuming, Eastern liturgies and Anglican divines, 1570–1662, *SCH* 13 (1976)

**X234.** M. H. Curtis, The Hampton Court conference and its aftermath, *H* 46 (1961)

**X235.** L. Damrosch, Hobbes as

Reformation theologian, *JHI* 40 (1979)

**X236.** J. Flaningham, The Occasional Conformity Controversy: ideology and party politics, 1697–1711, *JBS* 17 (1977–8)

**X237.** A. Fletcher, Concern for renewal in the Root and Branch debates of 1641, *SCH* 14 (1977)

**X238.** A. Fletcher, Factionalism in town and countryside: the significance of puritanism and Arminianism, *SCH* 16 (1979)

**X239.** O. W. Furley, The pope burning processions of the late 17th century, *H* 44 (1959)

**X240.** C. H. George, English Calvinist thought on usury, 1600–1640, *JHI* 18 (1957)

**X241.** G. E. Gorman, A Laudian attempt to 'tune the pulpit': Peter Heylyn and his sermon against the Feofees of the Impropriations, *JRH* 8 (1974–5)

**X242.** R. L. Greaves, John Bunyan and covenant thought in the 17th century, *ChH* 36 (1967)

**X243.** I. M. Green, The persecution of 'scandalous' and 'malignant' parish clergy during the English civil war, *EHR* 94 (1979)

**X244.** B. Hall, Puritanism – the problem of definition, *SCH* 2 (1964)

**X245.** W. Haller, Milton and the protestant ethic, *JBS* 1 (1961)

**X246.** J. E. C. Hill, Puritans and 'the dark corners of the land', *TRHS* 13 (1963) [see **54**]

**X247.** J. E. C. Hill, Seventeenth-century English society and Sabbatarianism, *B&N* 2 (1964)

**X248.** H. Horwitz, Protestant reconciliation in the Exclusion Crisis, *JEccH* 15 (1964)

**X249.** J. J. Hurwich, The social origins of the early Quakers, *PP* 48 (1970)

**X250.** J. J. Hurwich, Dissent and Catholicism in English society: a study of Warwickshire, 1660–1720, *JBS* 16 (1976)

**X251.** J. J. Hurwich, 'A fanatick town': the political influence of dissenters in Coventry 1660–1720, *MH* 4 (1978)

**X252.** G. Juretic, Digger no millenarian: the revolutionizing of Gerrard Winstanley, *JHI* 36 (1975)

**X253.** O. B. Kalu, Bishops and puritans in early Jacobean England, *ChH* 45 (1976)

**X254.** O. B. Kalu, Continuity in change: bishops of London and religious dissent in early Stuart England, *JBS* 18 (1978)

**X255.** L. Kaplan, English civil war politics and the religious settlement, *ChH* 41 (1972)

**X256.** H. F. Kearney, Ecclesiastical politics and the counter-reformation in Ireland, 1618–1648, *JEccH* 11 (1970)

**X257.** P. King, The episcopate during the civil wars, *EHR* 83 (1968)

**X258.** P. King, Reasons for the abolition of the Book of Common Prayer in 1645, *JEccH* 21 (1970)

**X259.** E. W. Kirby, The English Presbyterians in the Westminster Assembly, *ChH* 33 (1964)

**X260.** R. B. Knox, The social teaching of Archbishop John Williams, *SCH* 8 (1971)

**X261.** W. M. Lamont, Episcopacy and a 'godly discipline', 1641–6, *JEccH* 10 (1959)

**X262.** W. M. Lamont, The rise and fall of Bishop Bilson, *JBS* 5 (1966)

**X263.** W. M. Lamont, Richard Baxter: The Apocolypse and the Mad Major, *PP* 55 (1972)

**X264.** K. J. Lindley, Lay Catholics in the reign of Charles I *JEccH* 22 (1971)

**X265.** D. Lunn, Augustine Baker and the English mystical tradition, *JEccH* 26 (1975)

**X266.** J. F. Macgregor, Ranterism and the development of early Quakerism, *JRH* 9 (1976–7)

**X267.** J. F. MacLear, Popular anti-clericalism in the Puritan Revolution, *JHI* 17 (1956)

**X268.** J. F. H. New, Oliver Cromwell and the paradoxes of puritanism, *JBS* 5 (1965)

**X269.** G. F. Nuttall, The Baptist Western Association, 1653–1658, *JEccH* 11 (1960)

**X270.** W. B. Patterson, King James I's call for an ecumenical council, *SCH* 7 (1970)

**X271.** R. Peters, The notion of the church in the writings attributed to James I, *SCH* 3 (1965)

**X272.** C. Polizzotto, Liberty of conscience and the Whitehall Debates of 1648–9, *JEccH* 26 (1975)

**X273.** J. H. Pruett, Career patterns among the clergy of Lincoln Cathedral, 1660–1750, *ChH* 44 (1975)

**X274.** B. Reay, The Muggletonians, *JRH* 9 (1976–7)

**X275.** B. Reay, The Quakers, 1659 and the restoration of the monarchy, *H* 63 (1978)

**X276.** C. Robbins, Faith and freedom (c. 1677–1729), *JHI* 36 (1975)

**X277.** C. Russell, Arguments for religious unity in England, 1530–1650, *JEccH* 18 (1967)

**X278.** H. Schwartz, Arminianism and the English parliament, 1624–1629, *JBS* 12 (1973)

**X279.** M. L. Schwartz, Some thoughts on the development of a lay religious consciousness in pre-civil war England, *SCH* 8 (1971)

**X280.** F. Shriver, James I and the Vorstius affair, *EHR* 85 (1970)

**X281.** W. G. Simon, Comprehension in the age of Charles II, *ChH* 31 (1962)

**X282.** P. Slack, The case of Henry Sherfield, iconoclast, 1633, *SCH* 9 (1972)

**X283.** T. C. Smith, The persecution of Staffordshire Roman Catholic recusants, 1625–1660, *JEccH* 30 (1979)

**X284.** H. L. Snyder, The defeat of the Occasional Conformity Bill and the Tack, *BIHR* 41 (1968)

**X285.** L. F. Solt, Revolutionary Calvinist parties in England under Elizabeth and Charles I, *ChH* 27 (1958)

**X286.** L. F. Solt, The Fifth Monarchy Men: politics and the millennium, *ChH* 30 (1961)

**X287.** J. C. Spalding, The demise of English presbyterianism, 1660–1760, *ChH* 28 (1959)

**X288.** R. Thomas, The Seven Bishops and their petition, 18 May 1688, *JEccH* 12 (1961)

**X289.** H. R. Trevor-Roper, The Church of England and the Greek church in the time of Charles I, *SCH* 15 (1978)

**X290.** P. Tyler, The significance of the Ecclesiastical Commission at York, *NH* 2 (1967)

**X291.** D. Underdown, A case concerning bishops' lands: Cornelius Burges and the Corporation of Wells, *EHR* 78 (1963)

**X292.** R. T. Vann, Quakerism and the social structure of the interregnum, *PP* 43 (1969)

**X293.** B. R. White, The organization of the Particular Baptists, 1644–1660, *JEccH* 17 (1966)

**X294.** C. Z. Wiener, The beleaguered isle: a study of Elizabethan and early Jacobean anti-Catholicism, *PP* 51 (1971)

**X295.** T. A. Wilson and F. J. Merli, The Naylor case and the dilemma of the protectorate, *UBHJ* 10 (1965)

**Economic history**
**(see chapter 7)**

**X296.** B. L. Anderson, Money and the structures of credit in the 17th century, *Bus. Hist.* 13 (1970)

**X297.** R. Ashton, Deficit finance in the reign of James I, *EcHR* 10 (1957–8)

**X298.** R. Ashton, The parliamentary agitation for free trade in the opening years of the reign of James I, *PP* 38 (1967) [debate 43]

**X299.** D. K. Bassett, Early English trade and settlement in Asia, 1602–1690, *B&N* 3 (1968)

**X300.** M. W. Beresford, The common informer, the penal statutes and economic regulation, *EcHR* 10 (1957–8)

**X301.** J. H. Bettey, The development of water meadows in Dorset in the

17th century, *AgHR* 25 (1977)

**X302.** C. R. Boxer, Some second thoughts on the Third Anglo-Dutch War, *TRHS* 19 (1969)

**X303.** Y. S. Brenner, The inflation of prices, 1551–1650, *EcHR* 15 (1962–3)

**X304.** S. D. Chapman, The genesis of the British hosiery industry, 1600–1750, *Textile History* 5 (1972)

**X305.** J. A. Chartres, Road carrying in the 17th century *EcHR* 30 (1977)

**X306.** K. N. Chaudhuri, The East India Company and the export of treasure in the early 17th century, *EcHR* 16 (1963–4)

**X307.** L. A. Clarkson, The organization of the leather industry in the late 16th and 17th centuries, *EcHR* 13 (1960–1)

**X308.** L. A. Clarkson, English economic policy in the 16th and 17th centuries: the case of the leather industry, *BIHR* 38 (1965)

**X309.** L. A. Clarkson, The leather crafts in Tudor and Stuart England, *AgHR* 14 (1966)

**X310.** C. Clay, The price of freehold land in the late seventeenth century, *EcHR* 27 (1974)

**X311.** P. G. E. Clemens, The rise of Liverpool, 1665–1750, *EcHR* 29 (1976)

**X312.** D. C. Coleman, Technology and economic history, 1500–1700, *EcHR* 11 (1958–9)

**X313.** D. C. Coleman, An innovation and its diffusion: the 'new draperies', *EcHR* 22 (1969)

**X314.** J. P. Cooper, Economic regulation and the cloth industry in 17th century England, *TRHS* 20 (1970)

**X315.** R. Davis, A commercial revolution? English overseas trade in the 17th and 18th centuries, *HAP* G 65

**X316.** A. W. Douglas, The East India Company's attempt to exploit developments in fashion, 1660–1721, *JBS* 8 (1969)

**X317.** J. E. Farnell, The Navigation Act of 1651, *EcHR* 16 (1963–4)

**X318.** F. J. Fisher, London as an 'engine of economic growth', *B&N* 4 (1972)

**X319.** M. W. Flinn, The growth of the English iron industry, 1660–1760, *EcHR* 11 (1958)

**X320.** I. Gentles, The management of the crown lands, 1649–1660, *AgHR* 19 (1971)

**X321.** I. Gentles, The sale of crown lands during the English Revolution, *EcHR* 26 (1973)

**X322.** R. B. Grassby, The rate of interest in 17th century England, *EHR* 84 (1969)

**X323.** R. B Grassby, English

merchant capitalism in the late 17th century: the composition of business fortunes, *PP* 46 (1970)

**X324.** R. B. Grassby, The personal wealth of the business community in 17th century England, *EcHR* 23 (1970)

**X325.** H. J. Habakkuk, Public finance and the sale of confiscated property during the interregnum, *EcHR* 15 (1962–3)

**X326.** H. J. Habakkuk, Landowners and the civil war, *EcHR* 18 (1965)

**X327.** H. J. Habakkuk, The land settlement and the restoration of Charles II, *TRHS* 28 (1978)

**X328.** G. Hammersley, The charcoal iron industry and its problems, 1580–1700, *EcHR* 26 (1973)

**X329.** C. J. Harrison, Grain price analysis and harvest qualities, 1465–1634, *AgHR* 19 (1971)

**X330.** B. A. Holderness, Credit in a rural community, 1660–1800, *MH* 3 (1975)

**X331.** B. A. Holderness, Credit in English rural society with special reference to the period 1605–1720, *AgHR* 24 (1976)

**X332.** P. G. Holiday, Land sales and repurchases in Yorkshire after the civil wars, *NH* 5 (1970)

**X333.** E. Hopkins, The re-leasing of the Ellesmere estates 1637–1642, *AgHR* 10 (1962)

**X334.** J. K. Horsefield, The beginnings of paper money in England, *JEurEcH* 6 (1977)

**X335.** W. G. Hoskins, Harvest fluctuations and English history, 1620–1759, *AgHR* 16 (1968)

**X336.** E. L. Jones, The condition of English agriculture, 1500–1640, *EcHR* 21 (1968)

**X337.** J. E. Pilgrim, The rise of the new draperies in Essex, *UBHJ* 7 (1959–60)

**X338.** W. B. Stephens, The cloth exports of the provincial ports, 1600–1640, *EcHR* 22 (1969)

**X339.** H. Taylor, Trade neutrality and the 'English road', 1630–1648, *EcHR* 25 (1972)

**X340.** D. Woodward, The Anglo-Irish livestock trade of the 17th century, *IHS* 18 (1972–3)

**X341.** D. Woodward, Anglo-Scottish trade and English commercial policy during the 1660s, *ScHR* 56 (1977)

**X342.** J. Yelling, The combination and rotation of crops in east Worcestershire, 1540–1660, *AgHR* 17 (1969)

### Social history
### (see chapter 8)

**X343.** A. B. Appleby, Disease or famine? mortality in Cumberland and Westmorland, 1580–1640, *EcHR* 26 (1973)

**X344.** A. B. Appleby, Agrarian capitalism or seigneurial reaction? The north west of England, 1500–1700, *AmHR* 80 (1975)

**X345.** A. B. Appleby, Nutrition and disease: the case of London, 1550–1750, *JIDH* 6 (1975)

**X346.** R. Ashton, The aristocracy in transition, *EcHR* 22 (1969)

**X347.** G. E. Aylmer, St Patrick's Day 1628 in Witham, Essex, *PP* 61 (1973)

**X348.** J. V. Beckett, English landownership in the late 17th and 18th centuries: the debate and the problems, *EcHR* 30 (1977)

**X349.** A. L. Beier, Poor relief in Warwickshire, 1630–1660, *PP* 35 (1966)

**X350.** P. Borsay, The English urban renaissance, 1680–1760, *SH* 2 (1977)

**X351.** R. Brenner, The social basis of English commercial expansion, 1550–1650, *J Econ H* 32 (1972)

**X352.** C. Brent, Devastating epidemic in the countryside of eastern Sussex, 1558–1642, *LPS* 14 (1975)

**X353.** J. Broad, Gentry finances and the civil war: the case of the Buckinghamshire Verneys, *EcHR* 32 (1978)

**X354.** P. Burke, Popular culture in 17th century London, *Lond. J.* 3 (1977)

**X355.** P. Clark, Popular protest and disturbance in Kent, 1558–1640, *EcHR* 29 (1976)

**X356.** C. Clay, Marriage inheritance and the rise of large estates in England, 1660–1815, *EcHR* 21 (1968)

**X357.** J. S Cockburn, Early modern assize records as historical evidence, *JSA* 5 (1974–5)

**X358.** J. P. Cooper, The social distribution of lands and man, 1436–1700, *EcHR* 20 (1967)

**X359.** J. Cornwall, Evidence of population mobility in the 17th century, *BIHR* 40 (1967)

**X360.** D. Cressy, Occupation, migration and literacy in east London, *LPS* 5 (1970)

**X361.** D. Cressy, Describing the social order of Elizabethan and Stuart England, *Lit & Hist* 3 (1976)

**X362.** D. Cressy, Levels of illiteracy in England, 1530–1730, *HJ* 20 (1977)

**X363.** C. S. L. Davies, Peasant revolt in France and England: a comparison, *AgHR* 21 (1973)

**X364.** M. G. Davies, Country gentry and payments to London, 1650–1714, *EcHR* 24 (1971)

**X365.** M. G. Davies, The country gentry and falling rents in the 1660s and 1670s, *MH* 4 (1978)

**X366.** I. G. Doolittle, The effects of the plague on a provincial town in the 16th and

17th centuries, *Med. Hist* 19 (1975)

**X367.** A. Everitt, Social mobility in early modern England, *PP* 33 (1966)

**X368.** J. Grant, The gentry of London in the reign of Charles I, *UBHJ* 8 (1962)

**X369.** R. W. Herlin, Poor relief in London during the Puritan Revolution, *JBS* 18 (1979)

**X370.** G. S. Holmes, Gregory King and the social structure of pre-industrial England, *TRHS* 27 (1977)

**X371.** R. Laing, Social origins and social aspirations of Jacobean merchants, *EcHR* 27 (1974)

**X372.** H. H. Leonard, Distraint of knighthood: The last phase, 1625–1641, *H* 63 (1978)

**X373.** A. Macfarlane, History, anthropology & the study of communities, *SH* 2 (1977)

**X374.** A. Macfarlane, Review essay: *The Family, Sex and Marriage, HTh* 18 (1979) [see **641**]

**X375.** R. Machin, The great rebuilding: A reassessment, *PP* 77 (1977)

**X376.** J. Patten, Village and town: an occupational study, *AgHR* 20 (1972)

**X377.** V. Pearl, Change and stability in 17th century London, *Lond. J.* 5 (1979)

**X378.** W. Prest, Legal education of the gentry at the Inns of Court, 1560–1640, *PP* 38 (1967)

**X379.** P. Roebuck, Absentee landownership in the late 17th and early 18th centuries, *AgHR* 21 (1973)

**X380.** P. Roebuck, Post Restoration landownership: the impact of the abolition of wardship, *JBS* 18 (1978)

**X381.** R. S. Schofield, Crisis mortality, *LPS* 9 (1972)

**X382.** P. A. Slack, Vagrants and agrancy in England, 1598–1664, *EcHR* 27 (1974)

**X383.** M. Slater, Marriage in an upper-gentry family in 17th century England, [Verneys] *PP* 72 (1976)

**X384.** S. R. Smith, The social and geographical origin of London apprentices, 1630–1660, *Guildhall Misc.* 21 (1973)

**X385.** S. R. Smith, London apprentices as 17th century adolescents, *PP* 61 (1973)

**X386.** S. R. Smith, Growing old in seventeenth century England, *Albion* 8 (1976)

**X387.** D. Suuden 'Rogues, whores and vagabonds'? indentured servant emigrants to North America, *SH* 3 (1978)

**X388.** L. Stone, The educational revolution in England, 1560–1640, *PP* 28 (1964)

**X389.** L. Stone, Social mobility in England, 1500–1700, *PP* 33 (1966)

**X390.** L. Stone, Literacy and education in England, 1640–1900, *PP* 42 (1969)

**X391.** P. Styles, The evolution of the Law of Settlement, *UBHJ* 9 (1963–4)

**X392.** J. S. Taylor, The impact of pauper settlement, 1691–1834, *PP* 73 (1976)

**X393.** J. Thirsk, Younger sons in the 17th century, *H* 84 (1969)

**X394.** F. M. L. Thompson, The social distribution of landed property in England since the 16th century, *EcHR* 19 (1966)

**X395.** P. Tyler, The church courts at York and witchcraft prosecutions, 1567–1640, *NH* 4 (1969)

**X396.** R. T. Vann, Literacy in 17th century England: some hearth-tax evidence, *JIDH* 5 (1974)

**X397.** J. Walter and K. Wrightson, Death and the social order in early modern England, *PP* 71 (1976)

**X398.** S. J. Watts, Tenant-right in early 17th century Northumberland, *NH* 6 (1971)

**X399.** K. Wrightson, Infanticide in earlier 17th century England, *LPS* 15 (1975)

**X400.** K. Wrightson, Aspects of social differentiation in rural England, c. 1580–1660, *JPS* 5 (1977)

**X401.** E. A. Wrigley, Family limitation in pre-industrial England, *EcHR* 19 (1966)

**X402.** E. A. Wrigley, A simple model of London's importance in changing English society and economy, 1650–1750, *PP* 37 (1967)

**X403.** E. A. Wrigley, Mortality in pre-industrial England: the example of Colyton, *Daedalus* (1968) [see **633**]

**Local history**
(see chapter 9)

**X404.** K. R. Adey, Seventeenth-century Stafford: A county town in decline, *MH* 2 (1974)

**X405.** R. Carroll, Yorkshire parliamentary boroughs in the 17th century, *NH* 3 (1968)

**X406.** D. P. Carter, The 'exact militia' in Lancashire, 1625–1640, *NH* 11 (1975–6)

**X407.** A. M. Everitt, The local community and the Great Rebellion, *HAP* G 70

**X408.** G. C. F. Forster, The North Riding justices and their sections, 1603–1625, *NH* 10 (1975)

**X409.** G. C. F. Forster, Faction and county government in early Stuart Yorkshire, *NH* 11 (1975–6)

**X410.** G. C. F. Foster, County government in Yorkshire during the interregnum, *NH* 12 (1976)

**X411.** D. M. Palliser, A crisis in English towns? the case of York, 1460–1640, *NH* 14 (1978)

**X412.** C. B. Phillips, County committees and local government in Cumberland and Westmorland, 1642–1660, *NH* 5 (1970)

**X413.** C. B. Phillips, The royalist north: the Cumberland and Westmorland gentry, 1642–1660, *NH* 14 (1978)

**X414.** W. A. Speck, Brackley: A study in the growth of oligarchy, *MH* 3 (1975)

**Cultural history**
(see chapter 10)

**X415.** W. H. Austin, Newton on science and religion, *JHI* 31 (1970)

**X416.** M. 'Espinasse, The decline and fall of Restoration science, *PP* 32 (1965) [see **42**]

**X417.** J. Frank, John Milton's movement towards deism, *JBS* 1 (1961)

**X418.** R. G. Frank, Science, medicine and the universities of early modern England, *HSc* 11 (1973)

**X419.** C. Hill, William Harvey and the idea of monarchy, *PP* 27 (1964) [debate 31] [see **42**]

**X420.** J. R. Jacob, Restoration, reformation and the origins of the Royal society, *HSc* 13 (1975)

**X421.** J. R. Jacob, Boyle's circle in the protectorate, *JHI* 38 (1977)

**X422.** H. F. Kearney, Puritanism, capitalism and the scientific revolution, *PP* 28 (1964) [debate 31]

**X423.** W. Pagel, William Harvey revisited, (2 parts), *HSc* 8 and 9 (1969–70)

**X424.** G. A. J. Rogers, Locke, Newton and the Cambridge Platonists, *JHI* 40 (1979)

**X425.** R. P. Ross, The social and economic causes of the revolution in the mathematical sciences in mid-17th century England, *JBS* 15 (1975)

**X426.** B. J. Shapiro, Latitudinarianism and science in 17th century England, *PP* 40 (1968)

**X427.** B. J. Shapiro, The universities and science in 17th century England, *JBS* 10 (1971)

**X428.** L. Sharp, The Royal College of Physicians and interregnum politics, *Med. Hist.* 19 (1975)

**X429.** L. F. Solt, Puritanism, capitalism, democracy and the new science, *AmHR* 73 (1967)

**X430.** R. B. Walker, The newspaper press under William III, *HJ* 17 (1974)

**Scotland, Ireland & Wales**
(see chapter 11)

**X431.** A. B. Birchler, Archbishop John Spottiswoode: Chancellor of Scotland, 1635–1638, *ChH* 39 (1970)

**X432.** J. Buckroyd, Lord Broghil and the Scottish Church, 1655–1656, *JEccH* 27 (1976)

**X433.** S. A. Burrell, The apocalyptic vision of the early Covenanters *ScHR* 43 (1964)

**X434.** I. B. Cowan, The Covenanters: a revision article, *ScHR* 47 (1968)

**X435.** G. Davies and P. Hardacre, The restoration of the Scottish episcopacy, *JBS* 1 (1962)

**X436.** T. M. Devine and S. G. E. Lythe, The economy of Scotland under James VI: a revision article, *ScHR* 50 (1971)

**X437.** G. Donaldson, The emergence of schism in 17th century Scotland, *SCH* 9 (1972)

**X438.** W. Ferguson, The making of the Treaty of Union, *ScHR* 43 (1964)

**X439.** W. Ferguson, The imperial crown: a neglected facet of the background to the Treaty of Union, *ScHR* 53 (1974)

**X440.** E. D. Goldwater, The Scottish franchise: lobbying during the Cromwellian protectorate, *HJ* 21 (1978)

**X441.** J. Halliday, The club and the revolution in Scotland, 1689–90, *ScHR* 45 (1966)

**X442.** C. L. Hamilton, The basis for Scottish efforts to create a reformed church in England, 1640–1, *ChH* 30 (1961)

**X443.** C. L. Hamilton, Scotland Ireland and the English civil war, *Albion* 7 (1975)

**X444.** G. S. Holmes, The Hamilton affair of 1711–1712: a crisis in Anglo-Scottish relations, *EHR* 77 (1962)

**X445.** L. Kaplan, Steps to war: the Scots and parliament, 1642–1643, *JBS* 9 (1970)

**X446.** M. Lee, James VI's Government of Scotland after 1603, *ScHR* 55 (1976)

**X447.** A. L. Murray, The Scottish Treasury, 1667–1708, *ScHR* 45 (1966)

**X448.** F. J. Shaw, Landownership in the Western Isles in the 17th century, *ScHR* 56 (1977)

**X449.** T. C. Smout, The Anglo-Scottish Union of 1707: the economic background, *EcHR* 16 (1964)

**X450.** T. C. Smout, The Glasgow merchant community of the 17th century, *ScHR* 47 (1968)

**X451.** D. Stevenson, The finances of the cause of the Covenanters, 1638–1651, *ScHR* 51 (1972)

**X452.** D. Stevenson, The radical party in the Kirk, 1637–45, *JEccH* 25 (1974)

**X453.** T. C. Barnard, Planters and policies in Cromwellian Ireland, *PP* 61 (1973)

**X454.** T. C. Barnard, The Hartlib circle and the origins of the Dublin Philosophical Society, *IHS* 19 (1974–5)

**X455.** J. C. Beckett, The Confederation of Kilkenny reviewed, *HS* 2 (1959)

**X456.** J. Bossy, The Counter-Reformation and the people of Catholic Ireland, *HS* 8 (1971)

**X457.** K. S. Bottigheimer, The Restoration land settlement, *IHS* 18 (1972–3)

**X458.** A. Clarke, Ireland and the general crisis, *PP* 48 (1970)

**X459.** A. Clarke, The history of Poynings' Law, 1615–1641, *IHS* 18 (1972–3)

**X460.** J. P. Cooper, Strafford and the Byrnes' country, *IHS* 15 (1966–7)

**X461.** J. Lowe, Charles I and the Confederation of Kilkenny, *IHS* 14 (1964–5)

**X462.** J. Miller, Thomas Sheridan (1646–1712) and his narrative, *IHS* 20 (1976–7)

**X463.** J. Miller, The earl of Tyrconnel and James II's Irish policy, 1685–1688, *HJ* 20 (1977)

**X463.** M. Perceval-Maxwell, Strafford, the Ulster Scots and the Covenanters, *IHS* 18 (1972–3)

**X464.** M. Perceval-Maxwell, The Ulster rising of 1641 and the depositions, *IHS* 21 (1978)

**X465.** T. Ranger, Strafford in Ireland: a revaluation, *PP* 19 (1961) [see **848**]

**X466.** J. G. Simms, The civil survey, 1654–6, *IHS* 9 (1954–5)

**X467.** J. G. Simms, The making of the penal laws, 1703–4, *IHS* 12 (1960–1)

**X468.** J. G. Simms, Dublin in 1685, *IHS* 14 (1964–5)

**X469.** J. G. Simms, John Toland (1670–1721), a Donegal heretic, *IHS* 16 (1968–9)

**X470.** J. G. Simms, The Bishops' Banishment Act of 1697, *IHS* 17 (1970–1)

**X471.** V. Treadwell, The Irish Court of Wards under James I, *IHS* 12 (1960–1)

**X472.** V. Treadwell, The House of Lords in the Irish parliament of 1613–5, *EHR* 80 (1965)

**X473.** R. E. Ham, The Four Shire controversy, *WHR* 8 (1976–7)

**X474.** J. G. Jones, Caernavonshire administration and the activities of the justices of the peace, 1603–1660, *WHR* 5 (1970–1)

**X475.** J. G. Jones, Bishop Lewis Bayly and the Wynns of Gwydir, *WHR* 6 (1972–3)

**X476.** J. G. Jones, The Welsh poets and their patrons, 1550–1640, *WHR* 9 (1979)

**X477.** W. O. Williams, The survival of the Welsh language after the Act of Union, 1536–1640, *WHR* 2 (1964–5)

**X478.** P. Williams, The activities of the Council in the Marches under the early Stuarts, *WHR* 1 (1960–3)

# ADDENDA

The following comprises six recent books I have been able to read since September 1979, and six books which, upon reflection, I feel that I ought to have included already. There are cross-references at the appropriate points in the text.

**A1.** M. Flinn, *Scottish Population History* (1977) contains a long chapter on sources and methods, and a 100-page chapter on the seventeenth century.

**A2.** S. Foster, *Notes from the Caroline Underground* (1979), a brief analysis of the social and intellectual background to the trials of Leighton, Burton, Bastwick and Prynne in the 1630s.

**A3.** G. P. Gooch, *English Democratic Ideas in the Seventeenth Century* (1898, 1967), mainly, but not exclusively, concerned with the period 1646–60.

**A4.** G. Huxley, *Endymion Porter: The Life of a Courtier 1587–1649* (1959).

**A5.** W. J. Jones, *The Foundations of English Bankruptcy* (1979), looks at legislation, commissions and conciliar activity, 1560–1640.

**A6.** R. Ollard, *The Image of the King* (1979), a refreshing study of the kingship of Charles I and II. Of greater interest than the prosaic recent life of the latter by A. Fraser.

**A7.** D. W. Petergorsky, *Left Wing Democracy in the English Civil War* (1940).

**A8.** J. F. Rees, *Studies in Welsh History* (1947), includes chapters on the first civil war in Glamorgan and Pembrokeshire and on the second civil war in Wales generally.

**A9.** R. R. Reid, *The King's Council in the North* (1921), a mainly administrative study of the Council from its origins down to 1640.

**A10.** P. W. J. Riley, *The Anglo-Scottish Union* (1978), a detailed study of the political manoeuvres leading to the Union, 1701–7.

**A11.** A. F. Upton, *Sir Arthur Ingram* (1961), an illuminating study of an unsavoury financial adventurer and the founder of a large landed estate. It is vital for an understanding of the deadening power of vested interest within the Jacobean court.

**A12.** K. Wrightson and D. Levine, *Poverty and Piety in an*

*English Village: Terling 1525–1700* (1979), is a major addition to community studies, stressing the cultural and political dimensions of the rise of the market economy, and chronicling the rise of a godly oligarchy of wealthy inhabitants. Terling is in Essex.

# INDEX OF AUTHORS AND EDITORS

Entries refer to the running number given to each book and article. Article numbers are preceded by 'X'.